RESTORING POWER

to **Parents** and **Places**

RICHARD S. KORDESH

iUniverse, Inc.
Bloomington

Restoring Power to Parents and Places

iUniverse books may be ordered through booksellers or by contacting:

iUniverse
1663 Liberty Drive
Bloomington, IN 47403
www.iuniverse.com
1-800-Authors (1-800-288-4677)

ISBN: 978-1-4620-4871-7 (sc)
ISBN: 978-1-4620-4872-4 (hc)
ISBN: 978-1-4620-4873-1 (e)

Library of Congress Control Number: 2011914636

Printed in the United States of America

iUniverse rev. date: 10/28/2011

Contents

Figures

Preface

The community development field has produced many innovations and exciting projects, and it has created fascinating models of practice. But it has lost sight of the fact that families have been so diminished as productive institutions that they increasingly cannot contribute what they must to ensure that good places—neighborhoods, villages, and other kinds of small geographic communities—can be sustained. After thirty-five years of practicing, teaching, and conducting research in the field, I believe this reality must be reckoned with. In this book, I strive for a positive-critical argument that lays out what viable, productive families do irreplaceably for communities and the forces that have cut into those capacities.

This is the book's second edition. The first version, which referred to the approach that I advocate as *family-based community development,* was written as a companion piece to my practice and teaching. I wanted to test the waters with friends, students, and colleagues for my notion of the productive family. I shared this concept in graduate seminars I taught in social work as well as in urban planning and policy, and I distributed it at my workshops in both Chicago and Ethiopia. I gained a good sense of what I was communicating well and not so well.

In truth, the first book was not the first time I had published some of these ideas. That really occurred in 1995 as I was finishing a stint on the faculty at Penn State University at University Park. With the support of the Pew Charitable Trusts, I wrote a monograph titled *Irony and Hope in the Emerging Family Policies: The Case for Family Empowerment Associations.* In that piece, I argued that family policies in the areas of health, education, employment, and so on treated families mostly as consumers, neglecting their productive capacities.

Shortly thereafter, I moved to Chicago and enjoyed overseeing a team of graduate students in social work who worked with a community development corporation in one of the city's Latino neighborhoods. They helped design a project explicitly devoted to community organizing with parents. My involvement with that project continued into 1999. Shortly after that, I directed a project out of the Illinois governor's office that funded a variety of initiatives engaging parents productively in schools and in the creation of rural and urban enterprises.

The above experiences affirmed in my thinking that the traction was out there for projects that would invest in families as producers. But the resistance I received from some faculty and students, as well as some practitioners, to the arguments about the productive family helped me understand where concern for the family was losing its hold in the field.

One point that makes it difficult to seriously keep productive families and community development linked is the controversial nature of what constitutes a family. Many students and colleagues get very animated over this issue, especially when one argues, as I do, that marriage is a critically important foundation for a productive family. Many single-parent families, moms mostly, are doing heroic things to raise their kids and support their households, but accepting this model of the family as a norm also accepts marginalized fathers as a norm. And ample evidence exists to show the problems faced by communities with legions of marginalized men.

One can imagine how this debate about marriage and the definition of family can derail any further conversation about the roles of families in community development! I believe that this controversy has hurt the field, because the field has simply punted the issue away, embracing virtually any type of household or group configuration as a family. The problem is, if anything is viewed as a family, then the term loses the precise meaning required for sound policy design.

In the meantime, traditional families have continued to weaken, even as new forms of community development continue to emerge. With this book, I want to say to friends and colleagues in the field that it's time to get serious about the productive family. If we want communities of place[1] to become more capable of educating children effectively, generating sustainable

---

1   Communities of place refers to the bonds, common goals, and other unifying factors reinforced by sharing a geographical space. It contrasts, for example, with communities of shared interest that transcend geography (the disabled community, the Italian-American community, and many others). In this book, the emphasis is on places such as neighborhoods, villages, small towns, or rural regions. This is similar to the way the term is used in the planning and community development field. See for example, Thad Williamson, David Imbroscio, and Gar Alperovitz, 2002. *Making a Place for Community: Local Democracy in a Global Era,* New York, NY: Routledge. For more on the linked meaning of community and place see chapter 6, Community for Children.

economic development, reducing crime, and so on, we have to make the build-up of productive family capacities more central to our work.

Instead of the term *family-based community development*, I have opted for *family-generated community building*. The latter phrase is more precise than the former in that it recognizes families as actors, as agents, and as sources of energy for community building. The field must embrace the productive and coproductive family.

This work has grown from my own practice and reflection as a professor and community development professional, but also from my practice and reflection as a father and husband. First of all, I thank my wife, Maureen Straub Kordesh, for her insights, emotional support, and editing over the years. Whatever strengths this book might hold as a piece of writing, it owes them to her.

I also must thank my daughter, Kathleen, and my sons, Timothy, David, and Gregory, for making my efforts to blend my work and fatherhood into such a joy. When they were young children, they saved me time and again from taking myself too seriously as a professional. As young adults, and in Greg's case, as a teenager, they now push and challenge me to continually refresh my knowledge and thinking.

No one in the field of community development has been more supportive of my efforts with family-generated community building than Professor Alice Butterfield of the Jane Addams College of Social Work, University of Illinois at Chicago. In recent years, I have been fortunate enough to test and learn about this approach in Ethiopia. I would like to acknowledge my friend and colleague, Mulu Yeneabat, for teaching me about family and community life in his country.

Finally, I would like to thank the editors and professional staff at iUniverse for their patient, diligent, soup-to-nuts assistance in creating this book.

Introduction

In order to progress successfully through all of their stages of development, children need to grow up in good communities. Good communities do not occur without viable, productive families. Community development must build the places that enable children to thrive.

Community development ought to be everyone's business: it brings about daily consequences for mothers, fathers, children, city planners, neighborhood leaders, policy makers, and citizens in general.[2] Parents affect their communities simply through the activities involved in motherhood or fatherhood. City planners devote their working hours to shaping communities through zoning deliberations, neighborhood designs, deals with housing and commercial developers, and comprehensive plans.

Neighborhood leaders—the heads of community development corporations, parish pastors, and block club presidents—provide a voice for citizens at the grass roots in projects staffed by planners or pushed by developers. Policy makers create the legislative and regulatory context in which community development takes place. All these stakeholders depend on and affect how communities form, decline, rebound, and attempt to solve their problems.

What is the "productive family"? It is the family that controls enough of its time and resources in order to do some of the following: grow its own food, prepare its own meals, operate its own business, teach its children, care for its sick members, maintain its house, create healthy living practices, establish its own faith practices, create a safe neighborhood environment, cultivate democratic civic habits in its members, create crafts and works of art ... and many other things that are good for its members and the community. Children raised in productive families learn to be producers themselves. Moreover, they learn that it is normal to participate actively in creating their own lives.

---

2   I use the term "community development" interchangeably with "community building."

Furthermore, community development is not only something in which everyone participates, but also is a field of professional practice and research.[3] The theories and methods that have shaped this field of practice do not explicitly recognize the importance of the productive family to the field's effectiveness.

This book introduces *family-generated community building* in order to help correct for this important oversight. Family-generated community building depends on 1) parents and the institutions they build, 2) the community's institutions, and 3) the decision-making processes in which communities engage. Its success also relies on state and local governments to coordinate their different programs so that they add value to community and family institutions.

While they cannot carry out community development on their own, individual parents and families must take the initiative in rebuilding the productive roles that over many decades have been ceded to schools, agencies, and business corporations. Most parents already struggle to do this in various ways, but they must be more conscious of the powerful forces working against them. Succeeding in this effort is entirely possible, and it can be aided by actions undertaken by communities and governmental bodies as well.

Communities, for their part, must create a stable ring of anchor institutions that support, rather than replace, the productive capacities of families. Such institutions include responsive schools, finance organizations such as banks and credit unions, community centers, and other local entities.

Moreover, communities in the civic and governmental domains must make their decision-making processes more open to, and reflective of, the interests of productive families. For example, if a community is undertaking a strategic review of its school system - and if it recognizes that families are indeed coproducers of education - then the planning meetings, hearings, committee assignments, and choice of leaders will demonstrate that awareness. The education *system* comprises the families and schools together, and not merely the classroom-based teaching carried out by professional teachers.

The viability of productive family institutions, the presence of healthy community institutions, and the vitality of the community's decision-making process also depend in part on the actions of state and local governments. Government policies and programs can either help or hinder family and

3   The community development field aims to strengthen the planning, decision-making, and organizing capacities of people in neighborhoods, villages, cities, towns, and rural regions and other geographic areas so that they can achieve their shared goals. Professionals in the field might be trained in a variety of disciplines, including urban planning, rural planning and development, social work, public health, business, or education. The author has taught in formal community development concentrations in graduate colleges of social work and urban planning.

community life. They can help in particular by taking what is referred to as a value-added approach to program implementation. Value-added strategies can make existing family and community institutions more productive and able to fend for themselves. Government programs can also help by streamlining what is now a confusing and fragmented labyrinth of programs and make them responsive to communities and families.

Finally, actions at the family, community, and government levels all require a kind of politics that respects small, productive institutions and their need to participate as relatively autonomous actors. A robust, renewed kind of populism is needed to give small, productive family institutions a legitimate place in local and state polities.

How This Book Is Organized

This book addresses the above points in ten chapters. Chapter 1 opens the argument by taking a positive approach. It articulates how, at various levels of community and society, family-generated community building can be furthered. These possibilities range from actions by parents to changes in policies that could be enacted by state and federal decision-makers.

Chapter 2 considers the history and the current state of the productive family. It traces the family's evolution from a producer to a consumer. It also examines what this has meant for children and parents.[4] Different racial groups followed different but interdependent paths in the United States that led them to the current situations faced by their families. African-Americans and Native Americans saw their family and tribal institutions directly attacked over many years, whereas European family forms evolved in a more subtle interplay with industrialization. These different paths led to results that are similar in some respects and different in others.

Chapter 3 moves from the historical analysis to a consideration of power and how it fuels the construction and destruction of productive parent roles. It examines the forces beyond the individual man or woman that help define his or her role as father or mother. It also uses power theory as a tool to illuminate how parents can acquire more leverage.

Building on the power analysis, chapter 4 discusses the goals and organizing processes involved in family-generated community building. This chapter presents a unique, layered model of community built around children and explains how community development strategies can help bring the

---

4   This material draws on my earlier publication, *Irony and Hope in the Emerging Family Policies: The Case for Family Empowerment Associations*, (University Park, PA: Institute for Policy Research and Evaluation, The Pennsylvania State University), 1995.

model to life in actual localities. This chapter then draws concrete implications for community-building practitioners—professionals as well as parents.

Narrowing our view from the general, then to the community, and then down to particular issues, chapter 5 focuses on three concerns that are particularly relevant to the productive family: the family's habitat, the family's education role, and the family's food production. Habitat encompasses more than housing—it must be utilized intentionally as a productive family asset. Education constitutes one of the core productive activities in which families must take part; properly designed and affordable housing is necessary for a family to teach. Food production—rural, suburban, and urban—stands as a largely untapped opportunity for empowerment. It can integrate and strengthen intra-family roles, improve diets, upgrade children's health, and help with control of the family budget.

Chapter 6 argues that building community around children is necessary to develop in them the capacity to have trust in others. It further defines the core elements of communities that nurture this trust. It argues that productive families constitute the essential, inner layer of communities that are good for children.

To further illustrate how important the community context is for the restoration of the productive family, chapter 7 walks readers through a detailed consideration of the various steps that communities take routinely to solve their problems. If productive families are to thrive, they must be integrated into their locality's way of solving its problems—how it identifies important community issues, how it sets goals, whom it involves on task forces, whom it chooses to implement actions, and what questions it asks of itself to evaluate success. This exhaustive discussion brings to the fore the many daily decisions that community leaders make to either engage families productively or to ignore them.

Chapter 8 drives more into the concrete manifestations of family-generated community building. First, it provides a practical vision of what a community might look like were this mode of community building taking place. Then, it delves further into practicalities by identifying the kinds of indicators one could measure to determine its impacts. It concludes by suggesting how governments at the local, state, and federal levels could make policies into useful tools for helping communities realize success.

Chapter 9 asks why family-generated community building is not already conducted on a widespread basis. Obstacles exist in the stifling and narrow policy debates that are common around the family issue. Moreover, powerful, entrenched interests in politics and business do in fact benefit, at least in the short run, when the productive abilities of families are curtailed. However, many openings do exist to make family-generated community building a more widespread occurrence.

Most importantly, families themselves keep trying to *thicken*, or to expand and enrich, their parenting roles; to build their own enterprises; to save their farms; and generally to empower themselves in the face of significant odds.[5] Commitments jointly made among individuals, communities, and policy makers can turn those odds in favor of families and help them build the lives that children need. As chapter 10 argues, a more vibrant, coherent populism would help stabilize productive family institutions amid the dominant institutions that are the legacy of progressivism and corporate power.

When is a role thick or thin?

Roles are thick or thin depending on how many tasks and responsibilities they entail. Thick roles create a broader range of possible interactions with others than do thin roles. For example, a father who works at home can construct a thick role that involves not only the work itself, but teaching and mentoring about the work that can be carried out with his children. Contrast such a situation with a father who works for many hours a day in a distant office or factory. The distance and time required by the work role preclude the intensive teaching and mentoring made possible by working at home. The role of father in the first example is thicker than in the second example in that it involves a richer mix of work and teaching. It structures deeper interaction with the children. Living apart from the children, as many fathers do, precludes the construction of such thick roles. With more mothers working away from home and more fathers absent from the home, the trend for many decades has been a thinning of the roles of mothers and fathers.

In the Argument's Background

The arguments contained here have been seeded over the years by a reading of literatures in a variety of fields. Let us consider these foundational views.

Many scholars have likened the social context in which a child grows to an "ecology," emphasizing how the health and growth of individual members are reliant on the viability of the community. David Popenoe, an expert on

---

5   David Blankenhorn's typology of fathers' roles represents an insightful approach. I first
     encountered the notion of a "thin" role in his book *Fatherless America: Confronting Our
     Most Urgent Social Problem* (New York: Basic Books), 1995.

the modern family, has coined the term *social ecology of childrearing*.[6] Initiated by Urie Bronfenbrenner, an ecological school of child development has exerted widespread impact on how public policies are designed and programs are crafted.[7] The notion of ecology has proven to be a spotlight that casts considerable light on the social contexts in which children grow.

This study is concerned with those elements of the social ecology existing around children that produce the goods on which their healthy development depends. The term *goods* includes physical necessities like food and shelter, but it also means education, health, civic habits, and personal capacities like the ability to trust, to love, and to defend oneself when threatened by harm.

The most important productive unit in the child's social ecology is the family. Given their deep, unique, and even sacred bonds with their children, mothers and fathers must play roles in the production of the above goods that cannot be adequately replaced by professionals, by friends, by substitute parents, or by others.

The productive family and the institution of marriage are inextricably dependent on one another. No matter how difficult or challenging it might be to make stable, expressly committed, life-long relationships more possible in these times, the only option, if good communities are to be built around children, is to find ways to make marriage in its various cultural and religious forms more attractive and durable. Stronger marriages will provide a basic social armor that families with children need to defend their boundaries, to be productive, and to contribute positively to community building.

The demise of the *productive* family began when its ties to land and small places were undermined by the industrial economy.

The *social* ecology is coextensive with the *physical* ecology: the productive family and its physical places are also mutually dependent. The whole process that led to the demise of the productive family began when family ties to land and small places in cities were undermined by the industrial economy. Even today, families can be more productive when they farm or garden. Their children are safer when they can make sure that their immediate neighborhoods are safe. Their lives are better integrated when work and other activities can take place in their homes, on their lands, or in their garages or sheds. *Place* matters for the

---

6   David Popenoe, *Disturbing the Nest: Family Change and Decline in Modern Societies* (Hawthorne, MA: Aldine de Gruyter), 1988.

7   Urie Bronfenbrenner, *The Ecology of Human Development* (Cambridge, MA: Harvard University Press), 1979; J. Garbarino, *Children and Families in the Social Environment* (New York: Aldine de Gruyter), 1992; for variations on Bronfenbrenner's original ecological model, see Alan Booth & Ann C. Crouter, *Does It Take a Village?* (Mahwah, NJ: Lawrence Erlbaum Associates), 2001.

productive family. In turn, communities of place are stronger when cared for and defended by productive families.

Yet, encouraged by public policies and the economy, our social evolution is taking us in directions that undermine the productive family and sever its attachment to place. Although how it happens varies by economic class and race, mothers and fathers have in fact been relinquishing, either by choice or by compulsion, their productive roles for many decades. As Popenoe explains, some social theorists have in fact legitimated this change by treating it as an inevitable consequence of social progress.[8] However, evidence is all around us that the social ecology of childrearing is threatened by what is now the extreme fragility of the parents' productive roles.[9]

It is no coincidence that as parents exit their productive roles in the family, the places in which children live become more unstable, fragmented, devoid of a coherent moral context for fostering healthy social habits, and—for poor children—even dangerous.[10] Schools, agencies, clinics, and welfare systems expand around them, sometimes in good faith hoping to fill the gaps, and sometimes arrogantly seeking to fully professionalize the responsibilities once filled by parents.

However, teachers, social workers, doctors, and therapists know that without significant parent involvement, their efforts will not produce good outcomes.[11] We see indicators that the systems run by professionals are struggling to make gains in effectiveness, even as they expand. This situation is perhaps most painfully evident in education where, despite the expansion of schooling into summers and the growth of after-school programs, standardized test scores remain stagnant and, for many low-income children, wholly unsatisfactory.

This is where the social ecology stands today: in a vexing, ironic situation in which parents have been crowded out of relationships with their children,

---

8   See Popenoe's discussion of the "decline vs. change" debate about the family. Popenoe, 1988, chapter 1.

9   Blankenhorn uses this term to describe the evolution of fatherless homes. Although motherlessness is not as widespread a phenomenon, entering the workforce in large numbers has by necessity thinned the roles of mothers as well. See David Blankenhorn, *Fatherless America* (New York: Basic Books), 1995, 12–17.

10   For an eloquent statement of this point, see Amitai Etzioni, *The Spirit of Community: Rights, Responsibilities, and the Communitarian Agenda* (New York: Crown Publishers), 1993, 134-135.

11   There are many studies that document the benefits of parent involvement in education. A host of websites has made them accessible. See, for example, the Michigan Department of Education brief, "What Research Says About Parent Involvement in Children's Education In Relation to Academic Achievement," March, 2002. See also National Center for Family & Community Connections with Schools, Research Brief, November, 2002.

in which schools and agencies desperately seek more parental support, and yet in which their expansion is partly responsible for the parents' not being in the roles where they are needed.

To be fair, it is not only the human services and education sectors that have thinned, or weakened, the roles of parents. Business corporations initiated the trend in the nineteenth century as they drew family farmers and shop owners into jobs at their booming factories. Detaching men from their families, communities, and places prompted cultural changes as well.

As the previously unified work and family lives of fathers split into separate worlds, a new mix of individualism and collective immersion was introduced. The individualism was prompted by detaching men from the family and the community. The mass consciousness, which resulted from individuals' identifying themselves with new large organizations, was fed by joining them to the factories, the mines, and eventually the unions. Neither the individualism nor the mass consciousness was good for a thick fatherhood.

Detachment from the home and attachment to the workplace pulled fathers out of the teaching roles that had been supported by the previously home-based work of farm or shop. Attachment to the factory—whose corporate owners usually cared little about the well-being of their workers' families—pressured fathers to compress their role further into mainly that of bringing home a paycheck. Given the inevitability of the economy to recession and its attendant mass layoffs, even the narrower breadwinner role was hard to maintain in a predictable fashion through periodic downturns, including the recent devastating recession.

In recent decades, new faces of individualism have emerged that have corresponded with a further thinning of parent roles and further erosion of family ties. According to Bellah et al., individualism so dominates the outlooks of many men and women that many have a hard time even discussing coherently their family lives in terms of commitment, community, or service. Indeed, even relationships with children are legitimated for how they further the self-fulfillment of the adult.

The decision to stay married often hinges on whether the relationship continues to provide therapeutic benefits to the individuals. In such an equation, divorce is always an option; living alone becomes more attractive owing to the flexible choices it provides. *Generativity*—the capacity to dedicate oneself at least in part to the needs of the next generation—diminishes, as does the interest in thick parenting.[12]

The National Marriage Project found that men in particular are increasingly averse to marital commitments. They wait until later in life to marry. They see more benefit and less risk from cohabiting than from marriage.[13] Another observer points out that the act of faith implied by a marriage now stands out as an act of defiance against changing cultural standards that diminish it.[14]

Given how thin fatherhood, motherhood, and family institutions have become, launching an ecological restoration project focused on children is now necessary. This book introduces a multilayered model of the community that is meant to provide a way of thinking about how to further this rebuilding process.

It is not a job only for individual parents. *Family-generated community building* seeks to build the productive assets, roles, and institutions of families in the process of making communities around children stronger. It does so by mobilizing political, economic, social, and religious/cultural institutions around the production of goods that children need.

Family-generated community building can be a critically important element of place-based community development. It can help to restore the metaphorical social ecology as well as the physical ecologies where children live. It can generate new approaches to creating healthy and respectful roles for families to play in this restoration effort.

It must be said that focusing on mothers and fathers does not deny the importance of all households in the social ecology of childrearing. Neighborhoods are not composed only of families who are raising children. They are often diverse places populated by people living alone as well as households that exhibit many different groupings of adult inhabitants. Good community building requires unifying, engaged activities drawing on the assets of all such neighbors. Nor does an emphasis on families pretend that

---

12   Robert N. Bellah, Richard Madsen, William M. Sullivan, Ann Swidler, and Steven M. Tipton, *Habits of the Heart: Individualism and Commitment in American Life* (Berkeley, CA: University of California Press), 1985, 85–112. Generativity is a marker for adult maturation, according to psychologist Erik H. Erikson, *Childhood and Society* (New York: W.W. Norton & Co.), 1963. Therefore, thick motherhood and fatherhood can facilitate not just the healthy development of children, but the full personal development of adults. A culture that impedes it actually impedes individual fulfillment.

13   Barbara Defoe Whitehead and David Popenoe, *Why Men Won't Commit: Exploring Young Men's Attitudes About Sex, Dating, and Marriage* (Piscataway, NJ: The National Marriage Project), 2002. The project is now based at the University of Virginia. For information, go to http://www.virginia.edu/marriageproject/.

14   Leonard Pitts, "Abundant Blessings for the Royal Newlyweds" (Chicago Tribune, April 28, 2011, p. 17).

families can raise healthy children without positive, working partnerships with formal institutions such as schools, agencies, clinics, and business corporations. It does indeed "take a village" to raise children.

It takes productive families to build healthy villages. School reforms, violence-prevention initiatives, community economic-development strategies, and other community development efforts still do not build productive family roles and institutions deeply enough into their approaches.[15] Family-generated community building addresses these missing elements.

---

15   Theodora Ooms, "Where Is the Family in Comprehensive Community Initiatives for Children and Families?" (Washington, DC: Family Impact Seminar), 1996. This paper examines the relationship between family functions and family, social, and community capital, and then considers how comprehensive community initiatives can better strengthen families and involve them in the community-building process. Ooms is one of the first analysts to apply a family impact framework to policy studies in a rigorous fashion.

CHAPTER 1

Hopeful Possibilities for Productive Families

Community building brings together citizens and organizations in a particular place to define and achieve outcomes for the good of individuals and the locality overall. These outcomes can include better health and education, the creation of wealth, safety, civility, and other desirable goods or services. Although the achievement of these outcomes is often attributed to the actions of formal institutions such as clinics, hospitals, schools, businesses, and local government or law enforcement, these institutions cannot accomplish these results on their own. If the community is to be truly viable, each of these good things must be coproduced by families in cooperation with neighbors, citizen groups, and formal organizations. Due to the necessity of local coproduction, community building depends on the presence and vitality of families.[16]

> Community development is the process through which people who live in and work in the same place work together to define their visions, solve their problems, and pursue strategies aimed at making their neighborhoods and towns healthy and stable.

Productive families provide many goods and services to communities. They deliver some benefits indirectly simply through the work of being families. Others they coproduce with community institutions. Families actually coproduce most of the good things that communities count on being delivered by schools, the police, libraries, mental health agencies, and even churches. When these goods and services are present in adequate levels, the adequacy is due to the joint production taking place.

---

16   This book addresses the importance of *productive families*, with a primary focus on those formed by mothers and fathers. The author recognizes that many types of households exist in which children are being cared for lovingly.

The family is in a state of flux globally, with traditional forms in decline, others emerging. Overall, nonfamilial households are increasing faster than households with families. The development of modern businesses, schools, and government institutions threaten productive capacities of families. For many of them poverty is also a threat, worsened by the loss of self-sufficiency. That loss has been exacerbated by economic forces that have devastated small-scale family agriculture around the globe.

Some modern trends contribute to the family's decline but could also help more resilient, productive families arise. Even as traditional productive capacities have been harmed, others have begun to emerge. It is possible to identify trends that families can follow in order to become stronger now and in the future. Identifying those trends makes it more likely that steps for helping strong, caring, productive families will emerge and be carried out successfully.

What is meant by a productive family? A productive family generates goods and services that benefit its own members, its neighbors, and the community at large. A productive family creates social goods such as dependable citizens, as well as economic goods—for example, a family moving business. Some of these products are more physically or economically tangible than others. A productive family engages in this generative activity as part of its regular way of life. These goods can be for sale, for barter, used only by the family itself, or just given away. Some goods, like a well-kept yard that increases the property value of the house, are byproducts of taking care of the home or children. Others, like food dishes for a block party or surplus vegetables from a garden, are intentionally created for use by people outside of the home.

Sometimes it can help to understand a concept such as the *productive family* by considering its opposite, the consumer family. The consumer family is serviced by others. It buys things rather than producing them. It hires others to solve its problems rather than take care of them itself. It contracts with other people or businesses to take care of its property, such as the lawn, the garden, or the house. The consumer family is also dependent on professionals or their service systems for dealing with its health problems, mental health issues, or spiritual issues.

Practically no families are wealthy enough to live solely as consumers. Obviously, few families are wholly self-sufficient and few families engage in consumption only. Moreover, consumption is a necessary part of any productive life. But the productive family for our purposes is one that engages in generative activity routinely in all domains of its life—economic, social, health, and spiritual—and engages in much of its consumption for the purpose of furthering its productive capacities through its family roles.

The Good Things Productive Families Do for Communities

Let us consider some of what families produce and how their generative activity yields secondary benefits for their members, as well as positive outcomes for the community.

A number of writers concerned about families have addressed the many benefits of the *family meal*.[17] The family meal—the routine gathering of family members around the table to share food and spend time together conversing—provides a rich example of how different productive activities intersect in simple practices and then generate benefits for family members and the community.

Obviously, one benefit of a family meal is the food itself. The mother, father, or other members who prepare dishes to be shared at the table have engaged in the creation of meats, vegetables, pastas, or other dishes that provide pleasure and sources of energy to those at the table. Assuming that the food is made from nutritious ingredients and is properly cooked, dietary and health benefits are also generated by this activity.

But the physical goods and benefits only begin to describe the production that is taking place at a family meal. Various types of social production take place through the preparation, partaking of, and clearing of the meal as well. For example, relationships are forged or strengthened through the joint activities of preparing and serving a dinner. One person might peel carrots or potatoes, another might strain the pasta, and yet another might blend and monitor a sauce. The person in charge of the meal might delegate these tasks in such a way that lines of communication and collaboration are built. When disputes or miscommunications occur, further deliberations are needed to manage them. Therefore, preparation of the family meal can produce social goods like cooperation, communication, and problem-solving skills while strengthening family bonds.

> The family meal is a productive institution unto itself. It organizes many types and levels of creative activity. It creates material goods in the food and drink, and social goods in the relationships, the prayers, and sharing.

People need to talk with one another while they are working together. Such conversation might address the cooking tasks at hand, or they might also

---

17   Kathryn L. Robyn and Dawn Ritchie, *The Emotional House: How Redesigning Your Home Can Change Your Life* (Oakland, CA: New Harbinger Publications), 2005, see especially chapters 24 and 28; Miriam Weinsten, *The Surprising Power of Family Meals: How Eating Together Makes Us Smarter, Stronger, Healthier and Happier* (Hanover, New Hampshire: Steerforth Press L.C.), 2006; Laurie David, *The Family Dinner: Great Ways to Connect with Your Kids, One Meal at a Time* (New York: Hachette Book Group), 2010.

be about catching up with one another's lives in school, work, or otherwise. Or, they might just be about having fun.

The recipes followed in preparing various dishes might be important to the family's cultural heritage. The table setting—from kitchen light to candles; table top to table cloth; Melmac to Grandma's china—might also reflect the family's ethnic or cultural background. Preparing and eating ethnic dishes can help reinforce the family's identity, build pride in its heritage, and evoke memories of elders who may have passed down the recipes. Thus, even the food and the arrangement of the table can generate social goods like cultural pride.

As depicted below, the family meal structures many interactions that yield social goods. Speaking and listening skills emerge as young and old converse. Cooperation is learned as a means to create a pleasant group experience. Patience is acquired by waiting for dishes to be passed from brother to sister to parent. Young people and older members internalize these goods, making it possible to share them through interactions outside of the home.

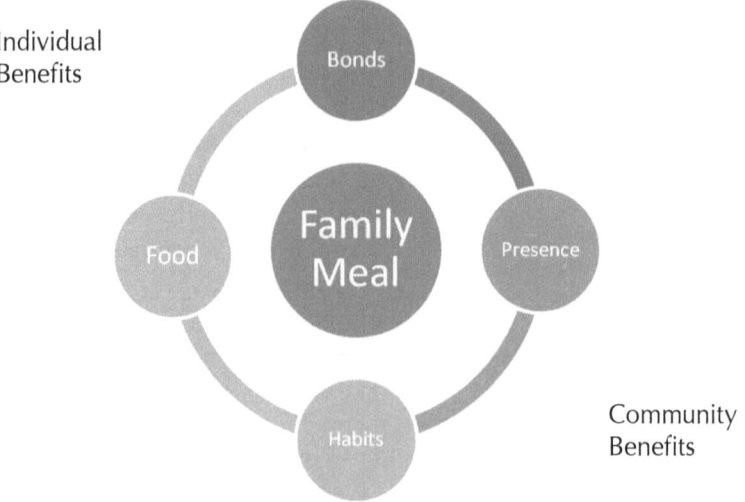

Figure 1: Benefits That Result from Regular Family Meals

Serving the dinner, including setting the table, plating the food, and other tasks can involve a number of coordinating and collaborating steps as well. There might be discussion of timing, deciding who will sit where and why, taking into account the kinds of seating required by small children, people with disabilities, or perhaps frailties associated with old age. Passing food and condiments around requires talk and hand-to-hand cooperation. Defining appropriate portions, especially when hungry young boys are at the table, might also generate conversation.

When the meal is not hurried, those at the table are facing one another around a shared, usually pleasurable, task of eating good food. The meal might be the only structured opportunity for all members to see one another face-to-face for any decent length of time. It encourages eye contact. If a parent or member with some seniority is able to encourage and manage the conversation, everyone somehow gets to participate. Children can compliment the preparers for the tastiness of the dishes. Family members can raise positive achievements or problems related to school, the neighborhood, or work. When the meal is finished, clearing the table and cleaning up can carry through the collaborations to the post-dinner phase.

Furthermore, this social production of relationships within the family does not end there. Through regular participation in a family meal, children learn many skills that help them behave positively and appropriately outside the home. They learn to converse, to share, to cooperate, and to do their part when it comes to helping out.

Parents at the table can find out what the children are experiencing in school or whether there are problems in the neighborhood that they need to discuss. Members can remind one another of events that might be coming up that require their attendance.

Just being home generates social goods. Consider that the whole cycle of preparing, eating, and cleaning up requires that family members actually be present in the home for a period of time. When people are home, their presence yields indirect benefits in and around the space of their habitat.

Being home increases safety around the home. Empty homes are targets of choice for burglars. Empty lots, unwatched stretches of blocks, or unmonitored alleys are magnets for criminal activity. Through their eyes on the streets, families contribute more routinely to preventing crimes such as burglaries or assaults that might take place near the homes. A kind of safe zone is cast around a home when its members are present. This zone lowers the likelihood of crime for the neighbors as well.

Thus, the simple practice of preparing and sharing a family meal creates numerous social goods:

Family memories are shared.

Stories are related.

Relationships are solidified.

Cooperative practices are learned.

Faith is reinforced.

Safety is increased.

There are many other examples of how institutionalizing certain productive activities in the family home yields a variety of direct and indirect, social and economic benefits for members and their communities. These include:

- Locating a **family business** in the home or making the home a place for work can encourage many, interrelated forms of economic and social production. Not only does working at home require the productive use and maintenance of space, it ensures the parents' presence. Some types of home-based work allow flex-time—working periodically in the day or evening—which also allows for home maintenance, cooking, coaching a child's baseball team, or coordinating with a spouse around the monitoring of homework.

- Growing a **vegetable garden or fruit trees** on the family property can set up a variety of shared tasks that build productive relationships among members. Tending the garden—fertilizing, composting, weeding, watering, pruning, and harvesting—encourages an attentiveness to the quality of the family habitat—the soil, water, birds, rabbits, worms, and other features—that would more likely be overlooked without it. The focus on landscaping, the quality of environment, and the production of food yields community benefits as well—sustainable use of resources, beautification of spaces, stable property values, and sometimes shared bounty from the garden itself.[18]

- Situating a variety of **schooling** activities in the home, for young children, school-aged children, or even older youth, is another way for the home and habitat to foster family production. Some families practice homeschooling. Others negotiate co-schooling arrangements with their school districts in which parents teach one or two formal classes at home. Some parents set up their own homes as preschool childcare centers and include age-appropriate educational activities as part of their offerings. Many parents create spaces in their homes that are set up for educational endeavors—rooms with computers, erasable boards, desks, tables, mini-libraries, and other educational amenities. In such spaces, parents are engaged in far more than so-called "family involvement" as an adjunct to formal schooling. They are coproducing education at least parallel with, if not in

"Family involvement" really doesn't go far enough. Parents must be coteachers rather than merely dutiful adjuncts to formal teachers.

---

18   For good examples of how parents can garden with their children, go to www. kidsgardening.com.

direct collaboration with, the formal teachers. This coproduction makes the family an institution that produces educational outcomes, social development, quality space in and around the home, and even helps the formal school district to achieve its prescribed targets for educational quality.

Families throughout the world practice these kinds of educational, business, and socially productive activities in a variety of forms and to various degrees. When one adds up all of the benefits that devolve to communities from them, one can begin to appreciate the enormous vacuum that forms in a place when many families cannot be productive. This hole in the community has grown larger as the productive capacities of families have diminished over time (see chapter 6 for a fuller discussion of these examples).

Trends That Can Strengthen Productive Families

It is in the interests of families to be productive: it lessens their dependence on corporations and public systems; it enables them to control to a degree their quality of life; it allows them to weather uncertainties and unexpected job losses caused by unpredictable employment markets; and it allows them to matter more in—and therefore to exercise more power in—the life of the community. There are trends shaping societies whose benefits can be captured in order to strengthen productive families. Some of these trends have and could continue to diminish family life if not harnessed appropriately.

Even as they have shrunk as a mainstream entity, in other respects productive families are reemerging in somewhat new forms. In particular, gender equality, technology, and the sustainable development movement have aided in the productive family's reemergence.

The global trend toward equality for women can diversify the kinds of contributions that women and men make toward productive family life.

The traditional roles of wives, mothers, and daughters carried many creative responsibilities—cooking, sewing, nursing babies, caring for children in the home, managing the home, beautifying the home, and other tasks. These tasks are as important as ever; in many cultures men and women still assume that they are primarily tasks for females.

However, with the relentless drive toward women's equality, these activities are gradually, even if in many contexts grudgingly, being taken up in shared fashion by husbands, fathers, brothers, and other men in the household. Greater opportunities for employment outside the home, as well as business and professional activities linked to the home, enable women to improve their economic contribution to the family and its habitat. Women can function as co-decision makers in arranging financing for the home and in determining major investments, they generate income for the family, they can teach their children about the skills and habits that it takes to hold a job or build a career, and they can draw on their broadening education to enrich their children's learning.

Women's liberation has often been derided as a threat to family life because it can foster careerism, pull mothers away from homes, or encourage a kind of "hyper-individualism" that steers young women away from considering marriage and family formation. Certainly, such outcomes have occurred. But it is not necessary that they must occur, given that the diversification of women's capacities adds to what they can bring to family life, especially in its productive dimensions.

Many men are growing with the diversification of women's capacities and learning to collaborate with them.

This trend is more evident in some cultural settings than in others. Indeed, in some countries it is still opposed officially by religious and government institutions. This lag between women's development and men's acceptance is real, and acts as a drag on the evolution of newer forms of stable, productive family practices.

Nonetheless, the global pattern is evident and relentless. Younger men in particular are growing up with women and girls who are assuming that their options for in-home and out-of-home opportunities are going to be broader than those enjoyed by women of prior generations. Many examples already exist of productive families governed by egalitarian relations between men and women. Thus, some men have already tuned in to the opportunities for themselves to expand their forms of production and expression within an egalitarian marriage.

Various forms of a fatherhood movement are helping to keep men engaged in defining and pursuing positive involvement with their families. Some strands of the movement emphasize the home and productive, egalitarian marriages. Not many iterations of the fatherhood movement in the United States speak outright about the benefits of a productive family and a productive family habitat at this point. Perhaps this is due to the fact that merely reattaching many fathers to their families at all presents a significant enough challenge.

Still, the intensity of the quest to define

The lag between women's development and men's acceptance of it is real in many settings, but the global trend toward the expansion of women's productive capacities is relentless and offers new possibilities for the productive family's renewal.

8

and support programs, policies, and individual decisions to engage men as fathers is a trend that can feed energy into efforts to strengthen productive families. After all, families can be productive in more ways and with better results when fathers and mothers are building them collaboratively and drawing on all of the capacities that they both possess.

In developing countries, many efforts at small-scale economic development are supporting home-based micro-enterprises through small loans and entrepreneurial training. This effort takes place even in the face of a severe decline in small-scale agriculture. In the United States, the documented numbers of home-based and home-linked enterprises are increasing, reflecting the advantages of linking residential and work space, as demonstrated by earlier forms of mom-and-pop shops with living space above stores and cafes. Moreover, many employers are allowing their workers to carry out their responsibilities at least in part from home offices. The expansion of communications technologies has detached many work tasks from particular sites of production. Homes and family habitats will continue to evolve as shared spaces for work and enterprise, thus providing the settings both for traditional and new kinds of production. The economic and social benefits from this evolution of the family home into a productive space can undergird productive families.

The sustainable development movement is encouraging an emphasis on the family habitat as a self-renewing, productive space.

Every activity that takes place in a home and every tool that can be used can be scrutinized through the healthy lens of sustainability. This perspective helps one begin to see how the habitat can be a place that conserves rather than merely consumes water. It lifts up possibilities for the home to generate rather than only burn energy. The urban farming branch of the movement demonstrates how on its own grounds, as well as in spaces shared with others, a family can grow some of its own food and avoid the more costly, consumptive activities required by grocery shopping. With the gradual adaptation of solar, geothermal, and wind technologies, the habitat of the family is slowly becoming a renewable energy producer and less of a *net* energy consumer. By capturing rainwater, for example, the family can use it in the garden rather than drawing on the municipal water supply.

There are some controversies in the implementation of sustainable development practices that clash with some productive uses of habitat. For example, burning wood or charcoal in developing countries is a widely practiced means of generating heat for homes. However, it also contributes to deforestation and the ozone layer's depletion. Affordable green technologies that are useful at the level of the habitat, such as passive solar ovens, will help to gradually lessen some of these conflicts.

Men, women, and youth throughout the world are learning entrepreneurial skills necessary for micro-enterprise development.

Small-business planning skills are more routinely taught in high schools now than ever before. The opportunity to work from home afforded by the Internet, and the necessity of working from home created by the instability of employment, has led many parents to take seminars and workshops in the various aspects of building a small business. Books and seminars about branding and marketing have become best sellers. In developing countries one finds nongovernmental organizations (NGOs), the United Nations, and government aid organizations offering such training to urban and rural residents. The finance industry has diversified to provide many public, nonprofit, and private sources of credit for such enterprises. The knowledge and skills gained by this training complement some of the other trends mentioned above—women's empowerment, the evolution of men's roles as fathers, and sustainable development—to make it more likely that family-based entrepreneurial ventures will succeed in the future.

Actions That Could Strengthen Productive Families

Given the above trends and the continuing importance of the productive family, finding ways to strengthen it is an imperative facing all societies. Fortunately, there are a variety of steps that individuals, educators, community leaders, and government officials can take to create a strong foundation for them now—and in the future.

Scholars and teachers can refresh high school and college curricula with positive perspectives on the productive family.

Home economics courses are now usually—and tellingly—called *family and consumer* sciences. This label reflects the trend toward viewing the family as a consuming institution. Such courses could be helpful in encouraging the support of productive family capacities. They do teach content that is already helpful in this regard—managing finances, operating childcare businesses, gardening, food storage, cooking, and nutrition. Why not create a course on the productive family by adding content on creating productive parenting roles, productive uses of home and habitat, the social and economic elements of successful family businesses, fatherhood as a productive, home-based role, growing food in small spaces, and creating balance in a marriage between home-based work and out-of-home employment?

Furthermore, other formal courses of study—family sociology, family studies, family policy, family counseling—could adopt a more balanced approach to considering the productive and consumptive dimensions of family life. Curricula in the human services fields have moved toward seeing families as consumers and clients, not as producers. Vast numbers of professionals are trained by these university programs each year. High school students graduate with mostly an exposure to the family as a consumer. More positive—including science-based—material about the productive capacities of families and their importance to individuals and communities would make formal schooling a force in supporting them.

Program designers can enrich curricula in family support, cooperative extension, family counseling, and premarital education with positive material about the productive family.

This concept refers more to training and service approaches adopted by professionals rather than college and high school curricula. There are many kinds of family support centers—church-based, school-based, freestanding, and others—that teach seminars, offer workshops, and provide booklets about caring for children, taking advantage of community services, and setting up mutual support groups of … mostly … mothers. These important programs could be bolstered by more information about the various ways that homes and habitats can be used to the family's benefit as productive resources. Such centers could also offer strategies and resources to support productive family networks.

Family support organizations can launch media campaigns infused with positive material about the productive family.

National and international organizations that work on behalf of families through service or policy advocacy could be enormously helpful in their media campaigns by lifting up and extolling the benefits of productive families. Steady media attention to this issue would be more likely if such groups stood behind such a campaign. A focus on the productive family can provide an inspiring frame around issues that arise in policy and cultural debates about children, women, fatherhood, and poverty. Media treatment of the family tends to foment a steady drumbeat of depressing news about family decline and the needs of families as overwhelmed consumers and desperate clients. A positive media approach envisioning better communities due to the presence of diverse kinds of productive families could help raise hope for the family's future.

Leading advocacy organizations and service organizations in the fatherhood movement can strengthen their communications and training material with models of productive, collaborative fatherhood and the formation of productive families.

In the United States, considerable resources are being devoted to the importance of fatherhood by organizations involved in the fatherhood movement. A productive, collaborative model of fatherhood could enrich the communication campaigns mounted by these organizations. Moreover, these organizations could illustrate the role of fathers in forming and sustaining productive families, and providing new kinds of hopeful images that would be complementary to the broadening roles of women as well as the sustainable development movement.

Churches, synagogues, and mosques can teach about the spiritual and economic benefits of productive families and egalitarian, collaborative marriages.

Whether they are Christian, Jewish, Muslim, or otherwise, religious congregations carry great moral and spiritual weight in establishing the kinds of family models that children and adults draw on as they envision marital and family life. The productive family and marriage are concepts with roots in all of these traditions. Some congregations are more likely to embrace an egalitarian model of marriage than are others. But if traditions that place men in the authoritative role are followed readily by all members, then the collaborative and productive family can still flourish. Through sermons, religious education, workshops, and other forms of communication, religious leaders can provide a strong moral force behind a positive stance toward the productive family.

School districts can experiment with broader varieties of co-schooling arrangements.

Children learn best in formal schools when they arrive with good study habits, language skills, familiarity with books, and an appreciation of the joy of learning. Thus, it is already well established that successful education is a coproduction involving the school and the family. Parents and schools can build on this understanding by diversifying educational methods to use more types of coproduction. Homeschooling is already an established approach. Co-schooling is also available, but not recognized as widely as homeschooling. In co-schooling, a family and a school agree that the family will teach subjects at home and the school will somehow recognize this learning formally. Accredited homeschooling curricula are available in core subjects such as mathematics, language, literature, social studies, the sciences, and humanities. Parents with the appropriate educational background can teach the basic subjects to their children at home, while sending them to school for other courses, as well as for physical education, laboratory work, music, and theater. Such co-schooling takes some of the burden off of the formal schools and solidifies the coproduction partnership with families.

The US Department of Education and other education agencies can fund experiments in co-schooling at the district level.

With more parents working from home and participating in flex-time arrangements, there is more potential emerging for co-schooling. With more school districts facing resource shortages and more districts confronting resistance to higher taxes, schools are looking to diversify their approach to education. The time is ripe for governmental education bodies to provide seed funding for innovations in co-schooling. There is a great deal to learn from this already-used concept. Seed grants should include evaluation funding in order to build up a reliable body of knowledge about methods of collaboration, types of subjects most amenable to co-schooling, types of students who benefit and how, the characteristics and capacities of families, and training for teachers and parents that might further it.

Local governments can reach out to local family businesses to deliver or coproduce some municipal services and goods.

Many municipalities in developing countries contract out or organize family-based approaches to delivering some services that developed countries consider to be the province of municipal employees or large companies. Such services include trash hauling, street cleaning, neighborhood cleanup, and the custodial maintenance of municipal buildings. Local governments could strengthen productive families by engaging them in service contracts or coproduction contracts in some of these areas. Other possibilities for contracting with family enterprises could include work as crossing guards at busy intersections, catering food for municipal functions, providing home-based child care for municipal employees, sorting refuse for recycling, monitoring playgrounds, organizing informal recreational activities, refereeing games in playgrounds, and many other types of activities.

The US Department of Housing and Urban Development (HUD) and other housing agencies can invest in more productive habitat design and construction.

HUD invests in the construction of many types of housing, including public-housing complexes, mixed-use developments, apartments for the disabled, scattered-site housing, congregate units for the elderly, and others. It also cofunds with other federal agencies' community development and planning projects that encourage the integration of residential neighborhoods with commercial and transportation amenities. Many housing agencies in countries other than the United States do the same. These investment programs could more intentionally encourage the development of productive family habitats both in the construction of individual housing units as well as multiple-unit blocks. Live–work designs for such housing have been available for some years, and some publicly subsidized developments have already employed them. Such designs make the flexible uses of space for residential and business activities easier by using more open rooms, higher ceilings, sound-proofed spaces, sufficient electrical wiring and Internet capacity, and even shared work spaces for adjacent tenants. Productive family habitats could also be encouraged by building designs that provide spaces on the ground, on rooftops, and in properly lit indoor spaces for residential urban agriculture. Moreover, sustainable development practices utilized in subsidized habitats could facilitate the conservation of rainwater, the production of passive solar energy, as well as community-based trash recycling and composting.

Centers that provide financial support and asset management services for families can integrate more guidance and assistance for productive families into their curricula and program content.

The quality of programs that help families protect and manage their financial assets has improved dramatically in recent years. Such programs are offered by community colleges, community development corporations, multi-service centers, workforce development centers, and local governments. In order to bolster productive families further, they could offer technical assistance to help families invest in and operate their own enterprises. The coupling of small enterprise training with some of these programs has already occurred in some cases. Making habitats more sustainable can further conserve resources and stabilize cash flow. Growing food with others at an appropriate scale can make good-quality vegetables less costly to acquire. Such centers might focus mostly on the important goal of helping moms and dads become employable. However, if they also trained other adults in the home for other, habitat-based capacities, this complementary effort could make employment outside of home for their primary client more manageable for the entire family.

Micro-loan programs should consolidate more expertise, guidance, and capital for productive family habitats and enterprises.

Low-cost seed capital for small enterprises is already becoming more available in the United States as well as globally. Along with this capital should come more guidance and targeted investments for enterprises that are created as part of the family habitat. Moreover, such capital should be flexible enough to support the integration of the spaces and functions for enterprises and the family's socially productive activities. For example, loans could support the renovation of home spaces that serve as offices during the day and children's playrooms during the evening.

The US Department of Agriculture (USDA) and other agricultural agencies should expand programs for, and shift some existing resources into, financial and technical assistance for productive family habitats that generate food.

As agriculture modernizes, small family farms that are transitioning successfully are those that create lucrative synergies among their different forms of production. For example, they manage to incorporate sustainable agriculture practices, target their production for limited market niches that the mega-farms don't serve effectively, become more attached to local communities and markets where locally grown food is valued, and diversify as businesses into a growing variety of eco-tourism and conventional tourism activities that capitalize on their agricultural activities. They also establish other businesses such as cafes, dog kennels, and mobile apiaries that move beehives from field to field, complementary to the farming. Many of these new business forms require training for family members and partnerships with other family farms in a region.

There are also a growing number of family and community gardening operations springing up in urban areas under various levels of guidance and support from local government and nonprofit coordinating bodies. Some set aside plots for family gardens and table spaces for family gardeners at community markets. The capacity to grow significant yields of healthy food crops in urban areas is gaining greater attention from planners and policymakers. Farming is gradually reestablishing itself in urban areas. This repopulation of cities and suburbs with family gardens, community gardens, businesses growing food with hydroponics, apiaries, and micro-farms on municipal lands is going to continue through the coming years. Each of these types of urban farms will be comanaged to a degree by families, along with individuals, couples, and small associations.

The US Department of Energy (DOE) should expand programs for, and shift resources into, finance and technical assistance for productive family habitats that produce and conserve clean energy.

From within the existing programs that encourage wind energy, solar energy, geothermal energy, and other alternative systems, a category of programs should be created for families and developers of family habitats that enable them to tap funds in the form of credits and grants. The technology exists to produce sustainable energy for a family habitat that operates a business, a small school, or a micro-farm. Both scale and simplicity are possible to ensure that family members can operate the equipment and teach their children about it. In other words, small-scale energy production technologies can be installed and operated to serve their direct environmental and economic goals, as well as the social goals characteristic of a family habitat.

The Time Is Ripe

This is a time of great challenge for families and the community institutions that need them to be viable. Many families are in crisis. Powerful social and economic forces continue to favor their destruction and the proliferation of nonfamilial households. Yet, communities and societies need productive families as much as ever. Some trends that seem to cut against family viability can also be shifted to support it. Encouragingly, there are many actions that all levels of society can take—individual, family, community, and government— that can feed on one another and make traditional and emerging forms of families more productive.

CHAPTER 2
The Productive Family: Past and Present

How did the productive family become such a threatened entity? Scholars in the social sciences and humanities have been tracking this devolution for some time. However, their findings have not always been interpreted negatively as indicators of social decline.

Indeed, the findings have often been defended as signs of societal progress.[19] This research began with the work of sociologists in the late nineteenth century, and continues through to some of today's scholarship by *communitarian* as well as ecological theorists. It documents the steady drain from the family's productive capacities in favor of professional organizations, agencies, schools, and business corporations.

While in part intended to improve efficiency and produce better social, health, and education outcomes for children, this expropriation of the nuclear unit by the larger community has gone far beyond a level that is healthy for kids. The power of formal organizations must be counterbalanced in ways that would create better communities around children.

Those communities need strong, productive family institutions, they need networks among those institutions, and they need healthy links between the family institutions and these formal organizations. Otherwise, these same organizations that have been responsible for eroding the family's productive

---

19   For example, especially early in his career, Emile Durkheim saw the family's role narrowing to such an extent that it would be replaced by the occupational or social group as a base for the moral development of children. American sociologists Ogburn and Burgess argued that the narrowing of the family's functions actually made the family more adaptable to large-scale social change. As they saw it, the family's personal functions increased its flexibility, even as its productive functions were replaced by expanding state and business organizations. Parsons saw the disappearance of family functions as a sign of its change, not its decline. See Popenoe, 1988, pp. 18–28.

functions will continue to do the same. Let us begin by recounting who drained the productive powers of families and how they did it.

From Economic Producer to Consumer

For the family, its change from producer to consumer took place slowly and in highly differentiated patterns. Economically, it happened in Europe during the nineteenth century in different ways depending on the industry and the country. Early periods of industrialization allowed for interesting new kinds of productive family enterprises to form. The trend away from production also took on different faces in the United States, depending on the region and whether a family lived in a rural or urban setting.

For example, the early industrial family in England was able to adapt to newly emerging business enterprises in the nineteenth century and contribute productively to it. Small numbers of rural families would form production networks, working with raw materials that were distributed to them by private companies. They were essentially contracted on an outsourcing basis, and families would organize themselves in groups to meet the production demands of the contractors.

The family participants in these proto-industrial structures had previously farmed their own properties, owned their own small crafts operations, or worked the land of wealthier landholders. Industrialization did not immediately draw them out of their rural communities into large factories. Rather, it enticed them to reorganize themselves into these productive networks that engaged in relationships with industry.

Factories were not at first productive enough on their own to meet the growth in demand for goods. Family workshops throughout the rural areas would take the raw materials from industrial entrepreneurs and produce finished goods. The goods would then be gathered by distributors working for the industrialists and taken to market or to waiting buyers.[20]

In some of the major emerging industries—textiles in particular—the reorganization of families into such proto-industrial networks was even accompanied by major role shifts between men and women. Women might be the primary production workers in the textile industry, whereas men managed productive activities at home.

For example, families in southern France practiced role reversal. Women carried out the labor, producing piecework for the glove industry. The

---

20   Martine Segalen, "The Industrial Revolution: From Proletariat to Bourgeoisie," in André Burguiére, Christiane Klapisch-Zuber, Martine Segalen & Francoise Zonabend, eds., *A History of the Family: Volume II: The Impact of Modernity* (Cambridge, MA: Belknap Press of the Harvard University Press), 1996, 381–382.

husbands, in turn, looked after the children and prepared meals. The women at times had to go into town to meet with the middlemen who negotiated their contracts and paid them for their goods. In this instance, one can see how the early organization of industry caused traditional arrangements in rural areas to be recast to fit the kinds of work demanded by the emerging industries.[21] In the face of industrialization, husbands and wives were altering their roles in order to maintain their homes as productive places.

Families wrestled with industrialization, fighting to integrate their intact relationships, including kinship networks, into the organizational machinery of the factory. Some factory owners complied by hiring family members in groups, by assigning them to the same work areas, by giving them preferences when it came to promotions, and through other means. Although such practices were later derided as nepotism, many industrialists sought to accommodate working-class family structures because doing so fostered productivity.

Families became identified with particular industries. They grew up in them, married within them, and formed communities identified with them. Groups of families would identify themselves by their trades. For example, as historian Martine Segalen points out, families in the weaving industry would close in upon themselves in their villages: "Setting up as husband and wife presupposed ownership of the tools of production, one or two looms."[22]

They needed their children to contribute to the family workshop or to maintain the home while the parents weaved. These kinship networks helped reduce the uncertainties posed by unpredictable trends in employment. When a man in one family could not work due to an injury or illness, a related family member working in the same weaving network could pick up some of his load. Or, were one weaver to lose a contract, the income (and the work) from a related weaver whose job remained steady could be shared.

Extended families helped their own members acquire jobs in the new businesses. Trade unions in England's cotton industries encouraged members to favor their own male relatives when recruiting workers. The tradition by which fathers passed their skills on to their sons, a common practice in rural areas, resurfaced in some industries. In major businesses in and around Paris, the reputations of employers were enhanced by high wages and an openness to letting family members pass on their jobs from one generation to the next.

These employers supported worker housing near the factories. Children would be socialized to identify with these employers. Marriages among workers within the same industries were often encouraged as well.[23]

---

21   Ibid., 384.
22   Segalen, "Industrial Revolution," 384.
23   Ibid., 392.

Wealthier families also adapted to industrialism: just as they had earlier passed on family estates, now they built their own firms and passed them on as intergenerational legacies. Some business organizations comprised two levels of productive family networks: the managing families and the working families. Thus, the displacement of family production by industrialization proceeded in a halting, sometimes contested, and differentiated fashion. Owners at times fought to hold families together as economic units even as they built new factories. But, over time, the tide turned in favor of nonfamilial business organizations.

Despite the efforts over many decades by families to adapt their productive structures to the changing economy, the trend in modern times has been to separate families from work settings, except in the case of enterprises created intentionally as family enterprises. Although many families start businesses, nearly 50 percent of such businesses close within five years. The industries in the United States that at first allowed the kinds of familial networks to work together in factories, such as those in France described above, have declined and shifted jobs overseas.

In the agricultural sector, the plight of family farms is well known. Corporate mega-farms predominate, and more family farms are sold every year. Thus, although the process through which industrialization dismantled the family's economic role looked somewhat different and proceeded at different paces in various countries, the overall effect has been a dramatic slicing away at the family's producer role and an expansion of its consumer role. This transformation served the interests of global corporations and state-owned industries. It slid families into narrow and increasingly disassociated roles within the nonfamilial systems that emerged.

Racism and the Destruction of Family-Based Ways of Life

Whereas for European families, the surrender of their productive functions to factories was in many cases gradual, for African-Americans and Native Americans, the experience differed sharply. Most Africans in the United States were exploited by a slave trade that tore them from their homeland villages, often separated them from their families, and exploited them as if they were barely human at all. The productive, familial, and village-based lives that they had been living in Africa ended for them the moment they became the property of traders and plantation owners.

Native American people had for thousands of years practiced productive family and communal lives in their tribes and among the smaller groups that made up their tribes. During the nineteenth century, when white farmers and small shop owners were fighting the battles against industrialization, they were simultaneously complicit in the destruction of the family-based, place-based communities that had been established by hundreds of different native tribes.

Thus, distinct from industrialization, white racism against black, brown, and red people in the United States acted as a malignant, destructive force that helped to destroy the productive, dense, family institutions that characterize tribal societies.

Industrialization evolved perversely in the United States through the slave trade. Even before the factories that emerged in the nineteenth century, African people were already being treated as agricultural machinery. Even though they worked long, hard hours in the fields and homes of slave owners, they also managed to form families, bear children, practice faith, and generally care for one another. But the slave system worked against these natural human impulses to build families and communities.

Although many owners of slaves contended that they did not break up families, evidence from bills of sale shows otherwise. Children were put on the market apart from their parents. Husbands were sold separately from wives. The family members separated this way were the ones most likely to run away. They fled to seek their spouses, their children, and, in the case of children on the run, their parents.[24]

Not only were their family lives in continuous peril, but their relationships were also exploited for the economic gain of the owners. Some slave owners became known as slave breeders. Some states benefited economically from the breeding of slaves.

One scholar tells how a planter in Virginia would brag about how many babies his slave women would produce. He was elated with the market value that a new slave baby represented. Because breeding slaves could generate such profits, slave girls were pushed into motherhood, often through rape, when they were thirteen or fourteen years of age.[25]

The money to be gained from *slave breeding* created another economic incentive for the owner to divide slave families. Even when slave families were advertised for sale intact, they did not always end up being traded as a unit. Owners often found that they could get higher prices when they sold family members separately. Many slaves were placed on the market as single individuals; this fact provides further indication that the slave system broke up families.[26]

After slavery ended, there were many instances of former slaves becoming

---

24   John Hope Franklin and Alfred A. Moss, Jr., *From Slavery to Freedom: A History of African Americans* (New York: Alfred A. Knopf), 2000, 204.

25   Ibid., 132.

26   Ibid., 133.

mobile, mainly in search of family members from whom they had become separated. In addition to searching for lost family members, blacks also sought to start their own farms, provide for themselves, sell crops on the market, and establish some autonomy for themselves from white landowners. However, many were without sufficient capital to purchase farmland. So, many worked as tenant farmers, paying rent to whites. Others worked as agricultural laborers, earning far less in the South than laborers in the North.

It was hard even for blacks who had capital to buy farms. Whites still owned the land, and land was a primary source of power.

Whites in the South who had lost their slaves embraced their land tenaciously as their only remaining economic asset. They resisted selling land to black people. They did not want them to acquire the capital, and therefore the power, that land represented. So despite the large numbers of freed blacks, the numbers of black-owned farms stayed small throughout the nineteenth and early twentieth centuries. Whereas blacks constituted half the population in the South in 1900, they owned fewer than 20 percent of the farms.[27]

In short, systematic racial oppression directed at African-Americans multiplied immeasurably the difficulties faced by their families, communities, and children. Indeed, their stories are unique. Industrialized racism established through slavery must be taken into account to explain the perilous conditions faced by their children today.

With the case of African-Americans, three hundred years of slavery constituted government-sanctioned, comprehensive attacks on the very institutions at the heart of family-generated community building: the productive family and family institutions. The slave–owner relationship violated the family's sanctity and the individual's dignity at the most fundamental level, and thus Africans and African-Americans for three centuries (except for the comparatively small numbers of free blacks in the North) faced a relentless, coercive assault on their basic productive capacities.

The abolition of slavery was followed by new forms of oppression that have interlocked historically to create an unending chain of racist regimes—sharecropping, "black code" laws in the South, housing discrimination in the North, and concentrated black poverty (twinned with concentrated white wealth) in all urban areas. These regimes have, on balance, denied African-Americans the space, resources, and capital needed to build the productive family institutions and solid communities around their children that have been comparatively more possible for whites.

Similarly, Native Americans formed another segment of the North American population whose family, community, and tribal institutions absorbed the brunt of the attacks by European governments and the United

---

27   Franklin and Moss, *Slavery to Freedom*, 307.

States government. The genocide practiced by European and American powers against the Indian tribes is well documented.

It was not the impersonal force of industrialization that undermined the productive family and communal lives of Native Americans—it was the fact that white people wanted their land, sought to apply their property laws to it, and endeavored to replace native cultures with a Christian, European culture. And they used treaties and military power to achieve these ends.

Native Americans had practiced preindustrial forms of family-generated community building for thousands of years on the lands that Europeans after the fifteenth century considered themselves to have discovered. Whether it was the desert tribes in the Southwest, forest-dwelling people in the East, or the plains tribes in the Northwest, the native way of life was one in which family, work, childrearing, and education were carried out seamlessly through thick, productive roles.

Children were educated not in schools but by their parents. As historian John C. Ewers's depiction of life among the Blackfeet people describes, the tasks of daily living provided the material for the daily lessons:

> The mother was responsible for the education of her daughters. The little girl began to learn about women's responsibilities by watching her mother and grandmother at their tasks. She imitated their actions in her childhood play. She began to help her mother in such light tasks as picking berries, and graduated to the heavier work of digging roots and carrying firewood and water for the lodge. As the girl grew older, she received instructions in dressing hides, preparing foods, making clothing, and in the women's crafts of geometric painting, porcupine quillwork, and beadwork.[28]

Since the Blackfeet followed the herds of buffalo in the Northern Plains, riding horses eventually became an important part of their way of life. It was an important work skill to be mastered by every man and woman.

Blackfeet children were accustomed to horses from infancy. As babies, they rode on their mothers' backs. At an early age, usually by their fifth year, they were taught to ride alone. The child was lifted into a high-horned woman's saddle on a gentle horse, and rawhide ropes were passed back and forth between pommel and cantle on each side and tied to prevent the child's falling. By the time children were six or seven years old, they were good riders.[29]

---

28 John C. Ewers, *The Blackfeet: Raiders of the Northern Plains* (Norman, OK: University of Oklahoma Press), 1958, 102.

29 Ibid., 103.

Fathers educated the sons, the future warriors and hunters who would defend their villages, raid others for horses, and secure the comprehensive source of food, tools, clothing, and other goods—the buffalo.

> Fathers looked after the education of the boys, but they were allowed much more freedom than were girls. They were encouraged to take part in rough, active body- and character-building games and sports. At the sun dance encampment, fathers pointed out to their sons the great warriors of their tribe and cited the honors that came to men who were brave and successful at the arts of war ... Boys of about ten were entrusted with the daily care of the family horse herd. The boy herder rose before daylight to go after the horses in their night pasture and drove them to a nearby lake or stream for water.[30]

Tied as they were to their land, native peoples across the continent suffered culturally as well as economically as they were displaced by European settlers. Forced on them were treaties that specified what lands would be theirs, how their lands would be used, how education methods would change, and generally how the people would assimilate the European ways.

Because the ways in which the families provided for themselves, educated themselves, and even identified themselves were so closely tied to their natural environment, the forced displacement and the obligatory cultural and economic rules shattered families. Not only were the economic means of production disrupted, but so were their cultural and religious means. Some treaties even specified that the United States government would back "Christianizing" the natives. The relentless move against the Native Americans' ties to their lands was therefore also an attack on their identities, cultural practices, and family structures. This severing of ties between culture and places cut deeply into the roots of productive family and tribal roles that had grown for many centuries.

Thus, three different and interdependent stories describe how families in the United States had their productive economic capacities stripped from them by those of greater power. During the nineteenth century, white families of European descent began to lose their productive functions to factories. Blacks experienced the decimation of their productive family capacities as a result of slavery and in general did not regain them after emancipation. Native peoples had them stripped away as their lands were seized and overrun by newly arriving settlers.

---

30   Ewers, *Blackfeet Raiders*, 103–104.

From Social Producer to Consumer

The process of industrialization did not stop with a transfer of the family's productive economic capacities. Modernization effectively industrialized education and social welfare as well. Even during the early nineteenth century, education reformers such as Horace Mann were advocating a diminishment of the family's educational role in favor of professional teachers. With respect to social welfare, the story demonstrated somewhat less of an intentional shift of power from families to nonfamilial organizations, but it occurred nevertheless.

Social welfare agencies grew in many respects to treat the problems caused by family and community breakdown, in particular, those ills precipitated by economic upheaval and the injustices described above. Let us consider the education arena first, then the social, and then the interplay among the economic, education, and social forces that produced the consumer family that is the standard today.

Allan Carlson argues that it was through education that the government initiated what has been a relentless attack on the family:

> In fact, from the very beginning, public school advocates aimed—as they had to—at undermining and displacing the family as the center of children's lives. The so-called "grandfather" of state education in America was Benjamin Rush, a Philadelphia physician, signer of the Declaration of Independence, and philosophical zealot and dreamer. In a 1786 essay, "Thoughts Upon the Mode of Education Proper in a Republic," Rush parted company from the education theories of Thomas Jefferson and described a different vision of learning. He began by removing the family from its central role, to be replaced by the government.[31]

Carlson holds that during the nineteenth century, the usurpation of the family's productive educational role was furthered by the Commonwealth of Massachusetts under the leadership of Horace Mann. The *Common School Journal,* founded by Mann and friends in 1838, featured the denigration of family life as one of its regular themes:

> —"[t]he little interests or conveniences of the family" must be subordinate to "the paramount subject" of the school (1841);

---

31   Allan Carlson, "The State's Assault on the Family," in Christopher Wolfe, ed., *The Family, Civil Society, and the State* (Lanham, MD: Rowman and Littlefield), 1998, 41.

—"Parents must cease to regard wealth as the best inheritance they can leave to their children" (1849); better that this family wealth be used to expand the common schools.[32]

Gradually, Mann's sentiments took hold state by state, and by the early twentieth century, mandatory public schooling had become a universal phenomenon. Parents—already reeling from the destruction of their farms, the demise of their small businesses, and in the case of Native and African Americans, more extreme experiences of oppression—had by the 1920s been displaced from the main educational roles in their children's lives.

A somewhat parallel expansion of government social welfare policies coincided with the growth of public schooling. Poor houses, mental hospitals, and orphanages were created in the nineteenth century out of compassion for those left destitute by poverty, the death of parents, or abandonment. Child welfare services emerged usually in response to child abuse and severe neglect. Juvenile delinquency programs were created in the early twentieth century by reformers such as Hull House's Jane Addams, who sought to divert youthful offenders from the adult criminal justice system. The massive increase in social welfare programs through the Social Security Act in 1935 again sought to provide cash assistance to families who had fallen into poverty owing to the death of a father or the disability of an adult. It was also introduced as an insurance measure to prevent the absolute impoverishment of the elderly.

Whereas a compelling case for each new program could be made based upon the evidence of each group's level of suffering, an ironic consequence for productive family roles resulted. Each service also added another layer of the state for families to contend with as consumers and another area of life in which the family would no longer serve as a producer. The most vulnerable families gradually became eligible for different benefits administered by myriad disconnected bureaucracies. Certainly, the welfare state addressed real problems; however, managing relationships with the welfare state became a full-time task for many families as it grew at the local, state, and federal levels. Dependency as clients transformed people—whose recent ancestors had been more self-sufficient farmers and craftspeople—into consumers of government services.

A significant postwar expansion of the welfare state took place after the Second World War when major benefit programs were created for veterans. These included veterans' hospitals, health insurance, education assistance, and low-interest mortgage financing. Further growth of the welfare state took place with the Older Americans Act in 1964 and the War on Poverty under

---

32   Ibid., 42.

Lyndon Johnson. Various provisions of the Social Security Act were amended to broaden the categories of people eligible for cash assistance. Public housing subsidies proliferated through the direct provision of housing units and rental vouchers.

By the 1970s, three clusters of citizens—the elderly, low-income mothers with children, and veterans—had become the main beneficiaries of the massive American social welfare system. Medicare, Social Security, and a number of programs funded under the Older Americans Act provided a ground floor of economic and social support for older people. Aid to Families with Dependent Children, Medicaid, and a vast number of social and health programs targeted the low-income segment of the population. In fact, a fairly substantial "underclass" of families contained many cases in which the same people received most of the services. A disproportionate number of the underclass were, and still are, African-Americans, Latinos, and Native Americans.

Leaders of the latter groups in particular have criticized social welfare programs—child welfare, cash assistance, and public housing—for disrupting family formation. Foster care systems operated with a bias against African-Americans, they argued, and led caseworkers and courts to prematurely remove children from their homes.[33] Many argue that "neglect" was in fact *poverty*, redefined as a condition to be treated through the removal of children from their parents. Until reforms were instituted in the 1980s, cash assistance was provided only to families with one parent, creating a disincentive against marriage and family formation. Public housing operated with a similar philosophy.

It is a fact that a notable decline in the marriage rate of African-Americans took place in the 1960s as the above programs were expanded. The general public concern about serving only the "truly needy" had helped lead to a pernicious bias against fathers among the poorest families, whose presence in the home disqualified their children from assistance. Thus, programs created to serve the poor instead furthered the unraveling of low-income families.

Family ties among the poor, who have been disproportionately black-, brown-, and red-skinned, frayed as a result of a long series of events. Acting interdependently with that unraveling were the changes that affected middle-class and working-class families, who have been disproportionately white. But it was the needs of an industrial economy that fed changes in education and prompted the growth of the welfare state.

The slave economy and the stealing of land from native people ravaged the family and tribal lives of Africans and Native Americans. Industrialization

---

33   Dorothy Roberts, *Shattered Bonds: The Color of Child Welfare* (New York: Basic Civitas Books), 2002.

was promoted by European powers, and it impacted European and American families by displacing them from their farms and small shops and relocating them into factories and modern business corporations.

The United States government created new social welfare and educational bureaucracies—the Freedman's Bureau for former slaves and the Bureau of Indian Affairs for displaced native people—and through these entities, sought to assimilate them into the modern culture that white people were creating. In turn, as waves of European immigrants arrived to work in factories, elite reformers in the United States also pressed for education policies that would socialize their children to become cooperative citizens and workers in the emerging industrial economy.

African-Americans, Native Americans, and immigrants all fought to a certain extent the social dislocation caused by economic change, but because of racism faced by nonwhites, the European immigrants generally found greater success. Many Polish, German, Irish, and Italian immigrants in turn-of-the-century cities managed over the course of one or two generations to amass savings, muster political leverage through local political and religious institutions, and basically navigate with reasonable success the new industrial and consumer economy.

Former slaves tried to acquire farms but did not possess the necessary savings. They sought to start family businesses, and many did, but many failed—again due to the poor buying power in ghettos as well as comparatively limited access to capital. They entered the industrializing cities of the North facing more discrimination and bringing with them less capital and political clout. Starting with less and facing more oppression at the onset of the twentieth century not surprisingly set the stage for African-Americans as a whole to enter the twenty-first century still disproportionately poor.

Industrialization displaced families of all races from their thick, productive family roles. Those who became the poor groups in the industrial world came to rely on poor-quality albeit universal education, in addition to surviving on the many different and fragmented programs in the welfare state. Universal education and the approach to welfare, as noted above, furthered the thinning of their roles. Those who became the middle classes in the industrial economy also saw their productive family roles thinned, but they were more able to cope with the trends because they had more money to buy goods and services.

The common experience shared by all families was one of displacement, a narrowing of parenting roles, and a conversion into consumer or client roles. The experience *not* shared by all was poverty, which still tends to be concentrated among black-, brown-, and red-skinned people.

Whether due to family breakdown among the poor or the modern work regimes of the middle class, children today do not see their parents work, and thus do not learn the skills and habits of a trade or profession from them. With most parents employed, a majority of young children will spend as many of their waking hours with hired caregivers as they do with their parents. The teaching of children that was a natural consequence of the home-based or farm-based work is now a rare occurrence.

The family-as-consumer is now the norm. It is not only material goods that the family consumes, but also the social services provided by others, including the service of childrearing. Middle-class families increasingly pay others to carry out many finely specialized tasks, including walking pets, mowing lawns, shopping for groceries, gardening, cooking, planning diets, providing personal advice on exercise routines, and cleaning the house.

The historical relationship to the production of food illustrates the general trend. The general trend has been as follows. Families have gone from:

1. producing their own food, to
2. purchasing food that they themselves cook, to
3. purchasing prepared foods that they only need to heat, to
4. paying other people to buy their food, and sometimes to prepare it for them.

Moreover, new businesses are growing that plan, prepare, and deliver whole meals to the home that follow planned diet regimens.

For those many families whose wages are not sufficient to "buy their way through" the situation caused by the loss of their productive capacities, it is not possible to pay others for such services. Working-class families struggle and incur debt in order to make ends meet. Poor families barely hold together at all.[34]

Resistance by Parents

Certainly, families themselves still fight to maintain many of the productive roles that a majority of theorists seem to say are lost forever. Since the mid-eighteenth century, families have resisted tenaciously the forces that sought to drain their productive functions. The powers behind those forces—business corporations, agribusinesses, government agencies, and school systems—have not completely wiped out their family-based counterparts. For example, family farms are in decline, but many are still adapting and

---

34   For further reading on theories of family poverty, taking into account the depletion of assets that many face, see Alice K. Butterfield, Cynthia J. Rocha, and William H. Butterfield, *The Dynamics of Family Policy: Analysis and Advocacy* (Chicago: Lyceum Books), 2010, especially chapter 5.

surviving; new family businesses open every day; and many family farmers struggle to reinvent themselves by focusing on different crops, specialized methods, or by embracing new business strategies.

Some public policies have even been reformed to halt the trend to transfer the family's roles. Government agencies in child welfare and income maintenance have started new approaches in recent years that check some of their tendencies to violate legitimate family boundaries. In fact, adoption and foster care provided by a child's relatives are more frequently preferred approaches to providing care for abused and neglected children.[35]

Other reforms are evident in education. Despite the expanding reach of public schools into morning, evening, weekend, and summer hours, there is also a growing homeschooling movement, as well as efforts made by many schools themselves to strengthen parent participation in their children's education.

For example, some schools have created parent resource rooms filled with literature and computerized information about parenting skills. Some put parents on the payroll to work as liaisons between the school and other mothers and fathers. Others are creating new roles for parents as mentors and tutors in the classrooms. Formal programs now exist that bring entire families into school buildings in the evening for meals and educational enrichment activities.[36]

In general, by limiting the time that parents have with children, as well as narrowing the range of activities around which parents and children interact, the overall trends have surely thinned the family's productive roles. However, they have not by any means eliminated them. The battle continues over how thick the family's productive roles should be. Because it is in their interest to do so, many families, even against considerable odds, open their own businesses; manage their farms; and even start new, unconventional enterprises aimed at

---

35   For more on kinship care in child welfare see James P. Gleeson and Creasie Finney Hairston, "Kinship Care as a Child Welfare Service: What Do We Really Know?" in James P. Gleeson and Creasie Finney Hairston, eds., *Kinship Care: Improving Practice through Research* (Washington, DC: Child Welfare League of America), 1999, 3–34.

36   Richard S. Kordesh and Robert Constable, "Policies, Programs, and Mandates for Developing Social Services in Schools," in Robert Constable, Shirley McDonald, and John P. Flynn, eds., *School Social Work: Practice, Policy, and Research Perspectives* (Chicago: Lyceum Press), 2002, 83–100; Joy Dryfoos and Sue Maguire, *Inside Full-Service Community Schools* (Thousand Oaks, CA: Corwin Press, Inc.), 2002.

giving them more control over their lives as families.[37] It is in their interests to do so because productive family institutions give them leverage against the forces constantly seeking to overrun their boundaries.

Linking the Loss of Productive Capacities, Family Decline, and Harmful Effects on Children

Not only is the drain on the family's productive capacities well documented, so are parallel trends that signal the family's decline. As productive capacities have been handed to formal institutions, divorce rates have risen, births out of wedlock have increased, single parenthood has expanded, and family formation itself is increasingly delayed or foregone altogether by young and middle-aged adults.

There is a wealth of evidence to show that children's problems on average worsen in divorced families, single-parent families, and situations in which unmarried couples cohabit.[38] Among the problems that intensify for the children are poverty, education failure, substance abuse, violence, and various health maladies.[39]

Are these two parallel trends—the change from producer to consumer and family decline—*causally* connected? Indeed they are.

The historical trend from thicker, productive roles to thinner, consumptive roles for mothers and fathers has made these people less dependent on one another. Spouses have been drawn into independent pursuits away from the family, and thus have become less able to defend their family's boundaries against the risks noted above. Multiplying their interests and responsibilities away from the family has diminished their ties with their children, as well as their own marital ties. Thus, weaker ties between spouses have led to higher divorce rates.

Some will object to this point, arguing correctly that the growing

---

37   According to Farm Aid data, there are about 565,000 family farms in the United States. Go to www.farmaid.org. [Last visited on December 9, 2005.] Joanne H. Pratt analyzed IRS data on home-based businesses. She found that between 1992 and 1999, the number of home-based businesses grew from 9 million to 10–12 million, a growth rate of between 11 and 33 percent. See Joanne H. Pratt, *Home-Based Business: The Hidden Economy: A Report from 125,000 Women, Men, Black, Hispanic, and Other Minority Entrepreneurs* (A study carried out for the Office of Advocacy, US Small Business Administration, Washington, DC), 1999.

38   Mary Parke, "Are Married Parents Really Better for Children?" (Washington, DC: Center for Law and Social Policy), Policy Brief No. 3, May, 2003.

39   For a recent study and careful review of literature on the effects of divorce on children, see Hyun Sik Kim, "Consequences of Parental Divorce for Child Development," *American Sociological Review*, 76(3), 2011, pp. 487-511.

independence of spouses from one another has been especially necessary for women, enabling them to emancipate themselves from the subordinate and, in many cases, demeaning and even abused roles that were common in marriages before the family's fragmentation. Less dependence for women upon men has liberated them to succeed in the economy, in professional circles, in politics, and elsewhere in ways that would not have been possible without the demise of the patriarchal family.

Clearly, women have benefited from the emancipating effects of gender equality. Men who desire more independently-minded partners have gained as well. So have children, especially girls, who grow from seeing their mothers succeed in ways not possible before the women's movement.

But, in a similar vein, there is considerable evidence that divorce, single parenthood, and the absence of fathers from children's lives have created stressful, often developmentally harmful upheavals in the lives of many children. Neither the male dominance that precipitates some divorces nor the isolation and chaos that can result from family dissolution is good for young people. Moreover, many mothers who also work are now struggling to restructure their work schedules to better accommodate their family roles. Many single mothers complain about irreconcilable and highly stressful conflicts between work and family.

Gender equality is a good thing for everyone, but it must become a stabilizing, rather than divisive, force in marriage. A new, more egalitarian and productive way of family life is needed. Even though many women and men know this, actually achieving it is an ongoing challenge.

Rebuilding Productive Families

In order for communities to be good places for rearing children, there will need to be a rebuilding of productive families, their institutions, and the practices that will sustain them. This rebuilding will by necessity take place under political, economic, and cultural conditions quite different from the preindustrial times that previously supported productive families. Among the factors that must differ dramatically are race and gender relations: equality will be paramount, and power will need to be mobilized on behalf of equality.

New ways to create thicker roles for mothers and fathers must be found. Thicker roles will require a reintegration of family in general and parental work roles in particular; thicker roles, by their very logic, require merging of previously separated dimensions.

In addition to thicker roles for individuals as parents, mothers' and fathers' roles will need to be reattached to one another. Children need for that to happen. Men must continue to become more deeply involved with children.

The only real solution is to rebuild marriage as a fundamentally egalitarian institution, and doing so will require, among other things, making motherhood and fatherhood into thicker, productive roles.

Building more productive capacity into the family will be necessary to give the family more control over its boundaries and its decisions. Thus, it is a matter of power, and strong partnerships between mothers and fathers—husbands and wives—are necessary for the empowerment and survival of the family.

Productive roles for families also create more opportunities for thicker roles, which in turn enable parents to be coproducers of the good things that their children need. Consider one small example: buying or growing one's own tomatoes. Growing tomatoes in a family garden does not simply "take more time," as a harried consumer-spouse might argue; it requires patience, planning, tending to plants, monitoring the rainfall, pruning, and harvesting. That is a thicker task than plucking a tomato out of the bin at the supermarket. But the thicker task creates more opportunities for enriching social interaction with one's children: teaching them about the environment, nutrients, bugs, soil quality, the process for making salsa, and other matters.

The productive family's beneficial effects go well beyond its own members. Communities grow stronger as well.

US Senator Byron Dorgan expressed well the positive social benefits of families whose productive capacities are realized through their farms. He referred to the "social product" generated by family farms, as opposed to corporate agribusinesses:

> The biggest costs of corporate farming may be social. We need to stop and ask what exactly it means to be "productive." What does a farm produce? A family-based enterprise such as a farm produces more than corn or wheat. It also produces a community. One might say it has a social product as well as a material product; and this social product is especially significant in a country that has more stuff than it knows what to do with, but less community and social cohesion than it needs … Jefferson was right. The kind of agriculture

we choose affects the kind of nation we are going to be. If we really believe that family and community values matter, how can we ignore the role of family-based enterprise in advancing these ends?[40]

Family enterprises, which require thick, productive roles for mothers and fathers, have long been central to the American vision of a free society. However, the historical trend has been to transform thick parenthood into thin parenthood, as well as to turn parents from producers into consumers. For the sake of children and ultimately the healthy development of adults, a rebalancing is in order—a restoration of thick motherhood and fatherhood, albeit with more equal, mutually respectful marital relationships—within the social ecology of childrearing.

---

40   Byron Dorgan, "Farms of the Future" (www.futurenet.org/14foodforlife/dorgan), 2000.

CHAPTER 3

Creating Productive Roles for Mothers and Fathers: How Does Power Matter?

As we have witnessed, power has been employed by businesses, professional educators, and government agencies to diminish the productive abilities of families. Turning this situation around in ways that make sense in the twenty-first century will require willful actions from parents, as well as support from communities and public policies.

The issue is rarely phrased as such, but whether a father's or mother's role is thick or thin can matter a great deal to schools, employers, religious institutions, marketing campaigns, and agencies. It matters because thickness increases the potential for productive activity in a role, whereas thinness complements a consumer orientation. A consumer orientation might make parents easier to manage, but in the long run, it renders them less effective partners in coproduction. The path to getting thicker roles would be eased for parents by laying out the terrain they must cover and the steps they can take.

Who Benefits from Thin Motherhood and Fatherhood?

Consider thick and thin roles for parents in education. One of the reasons that homeschooling and parent-run charter schools are controversial is they create thick educational roles for parents and thinner roles for professional teachers.

Or take the situation in a business. Thick parent roles can challenge an employer's desire to have employees who are not distracted from work by demands that arise from parenthood. Real employers vary in their levels of support for parents who need to take off time to attend to children's needs. There is a vast literature about the challenges of achieving a balance between work and family because this power struggle is constantly in play.

A similar confrontation over power can take place in the seemingly benign setting of a church or temple. Professional clergy sometimes find passive, dutiful congregation members easier to deal with than forceful mothers and fathers who center their religious lives in their homes. Such members might enter into a relationship with the church from an independent standpoint that doesn't accept at face value everything put forth in the Saturday or Sunday sermon.

Thick parenthood can be a threat to corporate marketing campaigns as well. Businesses target youth directly with their ads, often intentionally bypassing their parents' moral filters. Practically every parent has had the experience of walking into a room where the children were watching a morally objectionable ad for a line of clothing, or a movie that the child would not have had permission to watch if the parent had sufficient control of the television. Thinner parent roles involve less monitoring of the materials thrust in front of children by advertising. In short, life can be easier for the leaders of formal organizations in education, religion, and business when parents take roles that are thin.

However, many parents now seek more control of their time and resources, and acquiring such control entails building thicker roles. It is no wonder that flexible hours are such highly-prized employee benefits. But parents don't usually have a framework for thinking about how to create the thicker, more productive roles that they want in the face of demands from these organizations.

Building thicker roles calls for the acquisition of power. Power is not merely a matter of doing what one wants; power is about getting others to accept one's goals and to behave differently toward you. We do not create our roles in a vacuum, but instead in our interactions and negotiations with others. In the context of motherhood and fatherhood, power is about creating the role one wants and also getting others who can shape that role to accept our terms.

Consider the many forces that can define the role of a father, as shown in figure 2. Take, for instance, the example of education. Schools—not fathers—determine curricula, hours of operation, grading standards, extracurricular offerings, and amounts of homework. Each of these items, however, helps shape the father's role.

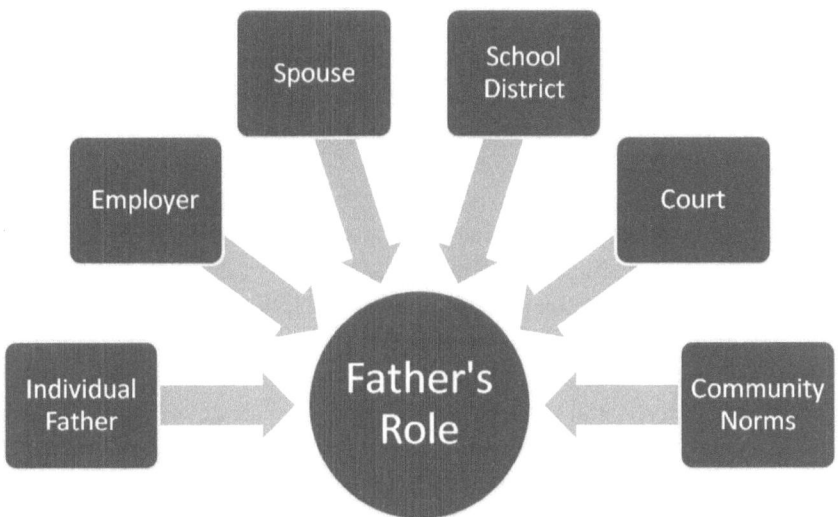

Figure 2: Who Defines a Father's Role? Not Just Dad.

For example, the school's history and literature curricula carry moral content that affects the belief systems of a man's children. The power to teach history—how one's ethnic or racial group was received in this country, why wars were fought, who were the heroes, and why revolutions took place—is the power to shape the minds of his children. Yet most fathers play little role in teaching history, even as an adjunct to what is taught in schools. The capacity to teach one's children has been defined to a great extent out of the father's role and into the teacher's role. The father's role as teacher has been thinned as a result.

One can see how the thickness of a parent's role partly determines the power that can be tapped through

Personal illustration: I had the pleasure of homeschooling two of my sons through seventh and eighth grades. One of our subjects in eighth grade was history. The text provided a vast number of facts and stories—such great triggers for meaningful conversation! The history text pointed out that President Thomas Jefferson related well to small groups but did not like to speak to large groups. Thus he did not follow the practice established by George Washington of addressing Congress in person. Just this simple set of observations about Jefferson led to rich discussions in our two-student classroom about leadership, relations between Congress and the president, how much politics has changed, and whether television has created a presidency that screens out certain kinds of great leaders before they would even consider campaigning. We held a history class three or four times per week. Each one generated probing, in-depth conversations.

that role. Were a father to teach history himself, as a homeschooling father would do, he would not only have more effect on what his children learn, he would also distance his role from the potential leverage that the school district would have over his role's definition.[41] The school district would lose some of its power as a result.

In fact, a father or mother, unknowingly or not, is engaged in a constant, multifaceted negotiation with many such forces in society not just over *how much time* he or she will have for parenthood, but also over *what will constitute* his or her parenthood. Courts determine how often divorced parents will see their children, under what conditions, and what precisely their responsibilities will be. (Divorcing families are common phenomena—their family boundaries have been shattered and their parent roles are in flux as courts often step into the crises to redefine the roles that the parties themselves are unable to renegotiate.) Employers determine how many hours parents will need to enroll their children in the care of others. Child welfare agencies often completely remove children from the custody of parents.

Surely, schools, courts, employers, and agencies all perform necessary functions in society. Families cannot do everything on their own. Divorces are not only caused by attacks on family roles from the outside, but by the failings of individual mothers and fathers. Child welfare agencies are necessary to protect children from abuse and neglect that is too often the fault of the individuals who are the parents. But, the point here is about power and roles: most mothers and fathers—people genuinely devoted to their children—have little capacity to enter and win the power struggles that today are causing family boundaries to be overrun and parent roles to be so thinned that for many children they barely exist at all.

Applying Power Theory to Motherhood and Fatherhood

As stated above, one employs power in order to change how another person or organization acts. A parent exercises power when she or he creates a role as mother or father and then influences those organizations to do what they would not have otherwise done for his children or community.

Steven Lukes, a scholar at Oxford University, devised an insightful typology of power that applies to our topic. Lukes argues that there are three ways of looking at power:

---

41   The statements about Jefferson in my personal illustration are from Daniel J. Boorstin and Brooks Mather Kelley, *A History of the United States* (Needham, MA: Prentice Hall), 2002, 179.

1. Situations of direct, observable, and conscious conflict (or negotiation) between two or more parties.
2. Situations in which one party is able to keep another party from pressing certain concerns by controlling the agenda or the terms of the relationship.
3. Circumstances where one party so dominates a situation that the weaker party cannot even recognize that its interests are being violated.[42]

To illustrate, let us consider how each view of power can surface in the relationship between parents and employers. In the first case, power is in play when a mother or father can negotiate directly with a supervisor about changing a benefits package in order to allow her or him more flexible hours. In the second case, the parent wants to press for more flextime but knows from having heard the supervisor's previous comments that even raising the possibility would put his or her employment in jeopardy; therefore, the parent would never even raise the concern. In the third case, a parent can't even imagine the possibility of flextime. He or she may not think it is appropriate to question the employer's policies. Or the parent may actually embrace the employer's view that the company's interests must come before the family's interest.

Similarly, one can see these views of power applying to relationships between parents and schools. The first perspective would be illustrated when a mother would challenge a teacher about the amount of homework her child is getting, arguing that by assigning so much of it, the teacher is encroaching on the family's ability to determine its own evening routines.

The second exercise of power would reveal that even though the mother would be aware of the harmful impact that the homework load would have on the family, she would be reticent to complain out of fear that complaining would hurt the child's grade.

The third view of power would be apparent if the mother is so in awe of the professional teacher, the teacher's credentials, or the school itself that she would not think to question the homework policies.

The above circumstances are easy to imagine because they are so commonplace, and so are many other instances in which a parent accepts a thinner role with his or her children owing to the power of an employer, a school, an agency, a movie production, or some entity. Collectively, there is so much role thinning taking place in the family that it is no surprise that families are in trouble.

---

42   Steven Lukes, *Power: A Radical View* (London: MacMillan Press), 1974.

What a Mother or Father Can Do to Reacquire Thicker, More Empowered Roles

There are steps a mother or father can take to create the more robust, productive role he or she wants, including:

- Being very clear about the desired role,
- Identifying the steps necessary to create it,
- Determining the obstacles one will have to confront to construct it, and
- Mobilizing the allied energies one will need to sustain it.

The following actions elaborate on the above steps, applying them as an illustration to the parental role of educator.

1. **Describe in as much detail as possible the current role.** What are the current activities involved? How much time is spent in the role? How often is one engaged in the role? To whom does one relate in the role? For example, in the role of educator, does the parent tutor the child on particular subjects? Does the parent teach moral or religious lessons meant to instill discipline or good study habits? Does the parent use his or her own work as a basis for teaching in some respect? Does the role mainly involve monitoring homework? How often: daily, once or twice per week, or less frequently? Which children does one relate to as educator—one's preschooler, one's second grader, or others? Does the parent build and draw on a home library or the Internet for educational resources?

2. **Identify the various people, organizations, laws, and other influences that currently make this role what it is.** How does one's spouse help determine the role currently played? Do teachers seem to favor active involvement on one's part, passive involvement, or none at all? Does the school seem to favor some of the activities that one engages in to the exclusion of others? What laws, government agencies, or court rulings might be partly determining the kind of educational role one is playing? Is one's time limited by the terms of a divorce settlement? Do the demands of one's job help shape the role now being played? How do one's own skills and educational background help determine the role as educator one is currently playing? What influences

might be shaping one's role through the demands and preferences expressed by one's child?

3. **Describe succinctly the thicker, more productive role that one wants.** Would the role involve more time? To do what? What would be the primary goal of this thicker role? What good things would be produced as a result of taking on this role?

4. **Identify the actions one must take to assume this role.** How would the role be built into one's daily or weekly routines? What new skills or tools might one need to carry out this desired role? How soon could one be ready to take the role? What explanation would need to be given to one's child in order to prepare him or her for the thicker role? What other roles—work, volunteer, friendship, or others—might need to be adjusted to allow for this fuller educational role?

5. **Conduct a *force field* analysis that identifies the people, organizations, laws, and other influences that will support and oppose these actions.** Identify the forces that would oppose one's assuming the desired role. Give a score of 1–5 to each opposing force, 1 representing a weak force and 5 representing a strong force. Do the same for forces that would support one's taking this role. Add up the points assigned to the supportive forces, and subtract from that the cumulative scores of the opposing forces. The result gives one a sense of the current supportiveness of one's environment for the desired role.

6. **Revise the action plan based on the force field analysis.** What oppositional forces might have to be persuaded or engaged in some fashion? Will legal action be necessary? What supportive forces might need to be utilized to lower the strength of particular, anticipated oppositional forces? What new, supportive forces might one need to bring into the situation?

7. **Initiate the campaign that will be necessary to create the role one wants.** Mobilize one's allies. Overcome or move around one's anticipated obstacles. Pull the legal or policy levers that might be available. Acquire the skills or knowledge one needs. Begin acting in the role and stay with it.

8. **Evaluate, learn, and adapt.** Acting in the role will provide new information about the supportiveness of the environment, as well as about one's own skills, emotional makeup, energy level, and resolve. Remap the terrain using the force field analysis periodically in order to stay aware of the shifting realities of power.

An Illustration: Building a Thick Educational Role

Figure 3 illustrates a hypothetical force field analysis: a framework developed originally by social psychologist Kurt Lewin.[43] In this case, a mother desires to thicken her productive educational role with her children. She is aware of several forces that impede her ability to take this role and play it as she wants. First, she works full time and knows that the demands of her clients or employer keep her mind occupied on the problems and challenges associated with her projects.

Second, she recognizes that her children are already receiving an education in history from the local public school and that this intensive course takes more of a secular, politically liberal view than does her own, which is a more socially conservative and religious perspective. Moreover, the history course is complemented by social studies and literature courses that are oriented similarly, and together they put considerable homework demands on her children. The time demands from the homework load, coupled with the biases of the curricula, make her feel "boxed out" of the teaching role she would like to be playing with her children.

Third, she is aware that popular media, such as MTV, music stations, teen magazines, and many movies carry messages that tend to diminish the intellectual aspirations of girls.

Finally, a fourth force aligned against her desired teaching role might be the peer culture of her teens that tends to draw them away from the family and into a sense that they are, as one writer puts it, a "tribe apart."[44]

---

43   Kurt Lewin, (Dorwin Cartwright, ed.), *Field Theory in Social Science: Selected Readings* (Oxford: Harpers), 1951. The figure below is original, but similar in some respects to many in the fields of consulting, organizational management, social planning and others that over the years, inspired by Lewin's scholarship, have depicted forces working for and against an actor's or institution's desired state of affairs. In this book, that state is a mother's desired teaching role. Rather than cite one of the diagrams developed by others who have applied Lewin's framework, I cite the source of the theory himself.

44   Patricia Hersch, *A Tribe Apart: A Journey into the Heart of American Adolescence* (New York: Ballantine Publishing Group), 1998.

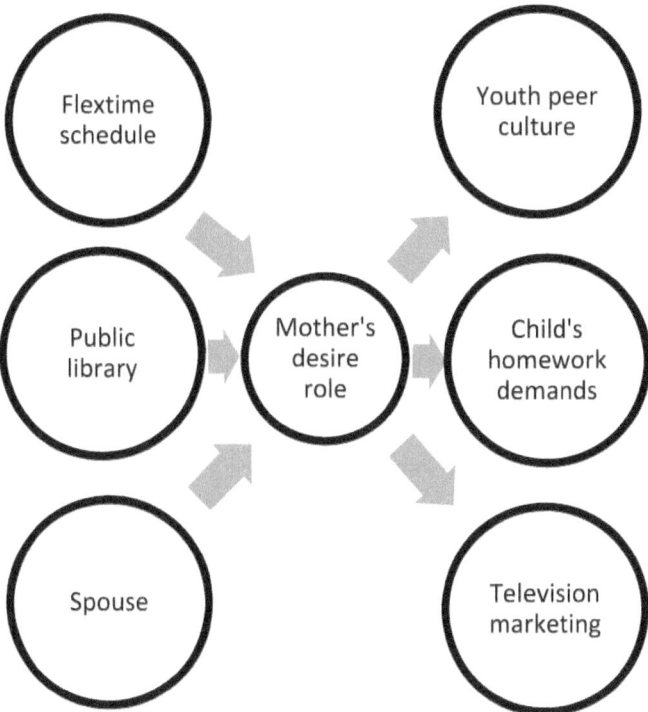

Figure 3: Push and Pull Factors For and Against Mother's Desired Role

Despite the forces aligned against her desired role, she can also identify forces that would be supportive. She is a member of a faith community that advocates strong parent roles in teaching faith and moral lessons. The public library would offer books, periodicals, and Internet connections to research data bases from which she could draw. She recognizes that she could press her employer for a flexible work schedule, or perhaps for a somewhat reduced weekly workload. She has identified a number of high-quality movies and documentaries that can be purchased, rented, or borrowed that she thinks her children would enjoy and learn from. Moreover, her husband would be supportive of all these actions and would like to thicken his teaching role as well.

The force field analysis would enable her to deal with the various faces of power that Lukes identified, as described above. It would reveal that there are instances where she will be able to confront an opposing force directly, as in the case when she would negotiate a new work schedule with her employer.

There are instances where she would have to get leverage when an agenda has already been set, as in the example of the public school's curriculum. There are instances in which her quest for power might be frustrated by those who would be unaware of forces acting against their own interests. An example of the latter might be other parents who are so intimidated by the professional credentials of public school faculty that they would not think to question whether the curriculum teaches something contrary to their own faith or cultural traditions.

The force field analysis illustrates that power does indeed matter. It matters with respect to all the roles that mothers and fathers must play if good communities are to be created around children. It matters with respect to the parent's role as a teacher or as a provider of healthy food. It matters to a mother's or father's role as a protector in a neighborhood. Power, then, is an important factor in family-generated community building.

Power and the Special Case of Men: The Current Crisis of Fatherhood

Restoring power to fatherhood is particularly important at this historical juncture because fatherhood is in a much more precarious position than motherhood. The number of children being raised in single-parent families is rising. The vast majority of those households are headed by mothers. Ever more men who helped to bring those children into the world are not living with them or their mothers. In expanding numbers, men have either been squeezed out or have opted out of active roles as fathers, especially in the context of marriage.

Power shifts are needed. But power will not be restored to the traditional, domineering role of father and husband. Women's development has already made any appreciable resurgence of that model untenable.

For men, this can be a good thing in that it opens up new possibilities for growth and personal capacity building. Many men have taken advantage of this historic opening. Others resist it. In some traditional cultures, many men have not been compelled to consider these new options. Still others remain confused by the role changes and personal development required by them. A collaborative *fatherhood* is needed to break the developmental impasse faced currently by men and boys; this stagnation holds back a needed surge of power into marriage and family life.

Productive Fatherhood amid Changes in Gender Power

As we have seen, like all parents, the role of father has been compressed over time by the expanding powers of schools, businesses, industrial development, and government systems. However, this compression has been particularly dramatic with respect to men's traditional powers as fathers, rooted as they were in agriculture, individual enterprise, and then the industrial economy.

Mothers' roles were compressed as well, but women have weathered this change more effectively; they have diversified their productive capacities, found more ways to stay positively engaged with their children and their communities, and have since made themselves more marketable with post-industrial employers. Whereas women have been more able to stay in the game of parenthood, men have more frequently left the game altogether due to a poor response to women's empowerment or an inflexible reaction to changes in the nature of work. Those who do attempt to create more balance between work and family life often find that employers and coworkers are unsupportive— even hostile—to their effort. Men have witnessed a disappearance of many forms of employment that they used to dominate. Thus, we confront the well-known statistics showing the decline of engaged fatherhood, the decline of marriage, and the rise, according to many, of the "unmarriageable male."

In short, the consumer mother and the consumer father are both thinner roles, but women more than men have found new ways to acquire productive leverage against the systems that would prefer to deal with them as consumers only. Women generally have fought harder against the thinning of their parenting roles. This is in part due to the fact that more men have lost their traditional roles entirely, whereas women have been able to maintain some of the traditional roles while building upon them. Yet, children and mothers need a productive fatherhood that can work with mothers, helping families thrive no matter how the economy changes.

What are the characteristics of the productive fatherhood now needed?

- A fatherhood that is engaged in a wider range of social as well as material production.
- A fatherhood that is productive in the home and family habitat as well as at a separate workplace.
- A fatherhood that blends production flexibly in the family, community, and work settings.
- A fatherhood that works collaboratively with mothers.
- A fatherhood whose productive capacities are renewed continuously.

- A fatherhood that uses communication technologies where feasible to work from integrated platforms that link his various life domains.

To be fair, traditional fatherhood involved social, as well as material, production. Men taught their children religious and moral lessons and the skills of their trades and crafts; they provided guidance through discipline, and used storytelling to convey the family's history.

However, these lessons and their resultant moral impacts were delivered largely in a context of dominant relations that were structured by cultural convention and by their role as sole or at least primary breadwinner.

A rethickening of the social roles of fathers is needed in order to establish a more diverse range of tasks. With the increasing absence of fathers and the thinning of the fathers' roles, even these types of social production have been diminished. In an emerging context of more egalitarian relations with mothers and shared responsibilities for generating income, there are more possibilities for social production by the adult men in the family.

Such tasks can include cooking meals, intensive child care, maintaining the home and outdoor habitat, caring for sick members, schooling children, and other responsibilities. Broadening the above functions provides the father more points of engagement with children around more issues and development opportunities than had been available to the traditional, full-time breadwinner.

Recentering one's work from the out-of-home workplace to the family habitat is now becoming possible again for men in many different kinds of occupations. In addition, with more mothers working for outside employers, fathers can work part time through contracting so that they can be present in the home more routinely.

Shifting work to the home with a flexible schedule, or with a part-time load, enables fathers to pick up some of the lost social production of traditional fatherhood and to expand into new forms. For example, fathers who are done working in mid-afternoon—three or three-thirty—can be home to provide teaching and structure for children after school. Or they can coach athletic teams such as baseball, basketball, or soccer.

It can indeed be difficult to find enough fathers to coach youth sports teams in communities where there are not many fathers present, either due to full-time, inflexible workloads or to a preponderance of households in which men are not active in the role of father. Yet, coaching opens up many of the opportunities for moral guidance, discipline, bonding, and team building that characterized the social production of traditional, thicker fatherhood.

Working in the home, at least part time, enables children to get closer to the substance and demands of the father's work, whether he runs his carpentry business from his home, teaches music at the piano, works on the Internet or, as a teacher, grades exams or prepares lectures. Having children close to the office or studio engages them more easily with what he does, why, how, and what it takes to be successful in his career. Children who can ask a father about his work while he is doing it are more able to internalize the lessons afforded indirectly through this kind of natural exposure. It also models for the boys a way of working that integrates it with his family responsibilities in practical examples that will make it easier for them to envision their own futures as working fathers.

The diversification of production for the father is, of course, enabled in part by the expansion of women's capabilities and roles. In the more egalitarian, collaborative marriages that are slowly becoming more common, there is a vast array of decisions and projects that can either be shared or delegated through mutual consent. Some mothers understand finance, accounting, legal matters, taxes, and other management issues as well as, if not better than, men do. This is the reality as women become solidly established in such fields as law, accounting, and management.

Rather than acting as a threat to men's power, this can be a reality that strengthens a productive marriage and family by freeing fathers to broaden the kinds of skills that they bring into planning collaboratively with mothers. Giving up some control over the family's finance decisions to one's wife might be counterbalanced by becoming more engaged in the planning of menus, the management of children's schedules, teaching, building a garden and growing food, and other areas of social production in the habitat. Overall, where the skills and knowledge of mother and father cumulatively expand, the family as a unit is empowered to manage more of its own affairs, and can make community institutions such as schools more effective. The collaborative marriage can increase the family's capacity to truly coproduce education with the local school. It enables the family to cogenerate safety with the local police. It empowers the family as a cobuilder of habitats that maintain property values and the overall attractiveness of is communities.

The power needed to rethicken these newly evolved roles of a collaborative motherhood and fatherhood can be accessed through an individual's own determined action, the relationship with a devoted spouse, and through ties with others families as well as with the broader community. Community building with and beyond the family is therefore necessary to confront the realities of power.

CHAPTER 4

What Is Family-Generated Community Building?

Community development cannot build the good places that children need in order to thrive unless strong and productive families are present. It may take a village to raise a child, but it takes viable, productive families to constitute a village. Community development will fail to achieve the goals of protection, education, and care for children unless it heeds the imperative to rebuild productive family institutions. Individual mothers and fathers cannot rebuild their roles and communities on their own. They will need to do so within broader efforts supported by planners, community leaders, and policy makers.

Family-Generated Community Building strengthens the productive capacities of families. It does so as it engages people in making their places unified and viable. In other words, it coincides with community development as the notion is generally understood, but also lifts up the importance of families as contributors to—not just beneficiaries of—the process. *Community building* is a process that engages people who live or work in the same locality in formulating goals, strategies, and desired actions aimed at bettering their places.[45] It is a process meant to build on and create unity among participants as they plan together and solve problems.

Family-generated community building is community development that lifts up the family as a central and necessary contributor to the process. It engages people in making their places viable and unified.

---

45   As stated before, "places" in this study refers to geographic areas that can become the bases for multi-functional (residential, commercial, educational, and others) communities—neighborhoods, villages, small comprehensive development districts, rural regions, small towns, and others. For an extended discussion of the relationship between community formation and place, see chapter six.

Goals

Family-generated community building emphasizes six goals:

1. **To build thick, productive roles for mothers and fathers.**

As a highly participatory process, community development engages people in solving their own problems. Family-generated community building engages mothers, fathers, and other critically important family members in examining their own roles and reconstructing them so that they have more power to shape their own lives, the lives of their children, and the conditions in their communities. A productive orientation is necessary in order to assume the proactive, assertive stances toward the home and the community entities that the parent has to build.

2. **To create diverse, productive family institutions.**

In order to be a good place to raise children, a community needs local institutions owned and run by families. These include family businesses and nonprofit enterprises. Productive family institutions can serve the community, but also their own members. Thus, a family that routinely grows some of its own vegetables, preserves them, and cooks them for its own meals has created a productive institution in its own household. If its garden is productive enough, it might share its surplus, barter it with other families, or sell it through local markets. A family might also take the lead in creating a neighborhood cleanup project. It could establish several days of the year when neighbors would work with the local refuse department to clean up empty lots or help residents who are disabled or elderly who need help with hauling trash.

3. **To establish communication networks among families, as well as among families and other community institutions.**

Families can become more productive if they are not isolated from one another in a community. They can also maintain more vigilance over the daily occurrences in their neighborhoods, as well as in schools, local businesses, and in local government. Communications technology now makes it more possible than ever for families and other community institutions to build community networks, keeping information about all kinds of vital matters flowing.

Schools, social agencies, and local government must demonstrate an openness to coproduction partnerships with families.

4. **To build host settings for family institutions into schools, agencies, malls, business districts, and faith-based institutions.**

If family institutions are to thrive and form effective, coproductive partnerships, then schools, agencies, and businesses must embrace them. Schools can host family communication networks on their websites. Commercial malls and business districts can create spaces for productive family enterprises. Faith-based institutions can serve as incubators for family enterprises, rebuilding their own ties with families and welcoming them as members.

5. **To engage families and community institutions in place-based community planning.**

Families, especially those with children, are perhaps more "organically" wedded to place than any other groups. They need and want their places to be safe, enriching, and well planned. They bring perspectives and attention to details that larger institutions and planners can easily miss, and thus it is in the whole community's interest to build them into the planning process. They will be more informed and equipped to do so if the four objectives above are also being met.

6. **To craft public policies that protect and support productive family roles and institutions in community development.**

Federal, state, and local policies can bolster productive family institutions directly and can make community planning embrace them more respectfully. Each level of government has a unique role to play in helping to realize this goal. State government in particular is emerging as a very significant potential asset in fostering family-generated community building.

Restoring Local Webs of Empowerment and Protection

Family-generated community building pursues the above goals by helping to build up the layers of family assets, family institutions, and community institutions around children in the places where they live. These layered assets are depicted in figure 4, a model highlighting the interdependence among children, their families, and anchor institutions in the community. The layered diagram depicts a web of empowerment and protection around children: it emphasizes the important roles of families as coproducers of the goods—both material and social—that children need in order to thrive.

Obviously, the threats and risks facing families today put children into settings that are not as safe or enriching as the diagram depicts. We will consider why the ideal is such a far cry from the reality in many places, but for now, let us examine each layer in the model, working from the inside out.

Mothers' and Fathers' Responsibilities:

The first layer around children is best provided by parents and the immediate, intimate sheltering and nurturing that they can provide to children. Although easily compromised in today's culture, marital vows can provide a foundation—a kind of social armor—bolstering the parent–child bond, the spousal bond, and the overall stability of the family unit. The vows help devote the spouses to their children, as well as to each other, and therefore ensure a flow of loving care and discipline that a child needs. Other commitments beyond marital vows also build this first protective layer around a child's development: a commitment to help a child succeed in school, a commitment to secure a decent home, or a commitment to support a child in sports or artistic pursuits.

Productive Family Assets and Institutions:

Vows, commitments, and love are more easily maintained by, and make it easier to build, the family's own productive assets and institutions. This second layer of the web of empowerment and protection is, therefore, interdependent with the first. Some institutions, such as family-owned businesses, can be organized formally. Other institutions, such as prayer and sacred rituals, can be arranged informally. Gardens can produce food for the family's own consumption or flowers for its enjoyment, or they can be grown as businesses or as parts of cooperatives in which families share their produce with one another. A house can surely be a productive asset, as well as a place for shelter and safety. It can be a place of business. A family farm is an institution through which a family strives to earn all or a good portion of its livelihood through agricultural production.

Any home can also be a school, even if the children also attend a formal public or private school. A family can institutionalize daily reading, educational games, watching educational television, or learning activities associated with the family's garden or business. Some families make their homes into productive places for music or art. More families are building their own websites to share their photos, poetry, business information, art works, and other things that they produce.

A family can best participate as a coeducator with the formal school when it establishes productive activities at home for its own children.

The family's various assets and institutions can be mutually supporting. Home ownership obviously makes it easier to operate a business out of the basement. A flourishing, productive garden is more possible when one can work from a home office and find break time to maintain it. A family can more easily function as a *coeducator* with the formal school when there are productive household activities taking place from which children can learn. Homes and neighborhoods are safer places when families are regularly present to carry out important, productive tasks in their own habitats.

Multifamily Institutions and Networks:

Families can better support fidelity to vows, as well as strong parent–child bonds, when they are linked with others who are similarly committed. A strong web of empowerment and protection around children, therefore, also must include institutions and networks that form healthy relationships among productive families, as well as with other households that might not consist of families.

Families are more likely to maintain their own faith practices when they are part of faith circles, home-based prayer or discussion groups, or small faith communities that meet in homes. Family farmers can barely survive in the modern agricultural economy without belonging to cooperatives involving other farmers. Some families not only maintain their own websites, but also participate in multi-household communication networks based on the World Wide Web. Many families come together and form friendships, as well as become more widely informed about their communities, when their children play on the same youth sports teams. Moreover, home-based business owners can form their own formal or informal networks that facilitate information sharing, training, and general emotional support.

Community Institutions as Hosts for Productive Families:

Obviously, children need more than families, and families need more than each other. The outermost local ring in the web of empowerment and protection consists of formal institutions. From the perspective of family-generated community building, these institutions are important not just for the goods and services that they deliver, but also for the mutually enriching relationships they form with productive family institutions. One critically important role that community institutions must serve is as a host for family institutions.

There are many examples of how formal organizations can host those formed by families:

- Community technology centers can host family-to-family e-mail networks and websites on their servers. They can help low-income families launch e-businesses from their computers.

- Schools can dedicate spaces in their buildings and places in their curricula for parents to play significant roles as educators, music teachers, directors of plays, and gym coaches.
- Community development corporations can host small businesses, helping to incubate them and providing initial space and phones in their start-up phases.
- Family resource centers can sponsor family-owned childcare cooperatives.
- Producers and energy cooperatives can host family farms and family-owned power generators—like windmills.
- Common interest communities (homeowner and condo-owner associations) can sponsor family-based child care cooperatives or home-based business support centers in their own complexes.
- Libraries can host home schools, including those that co-teach their children with formal schools and those that teach children at home entirely.
- Congregations and parishes can host family prayer and home-based discussions.
- Museums can host exhibits and workshops that teach about the cultural roots of various family traditions.

When seen together, as depicted in figure 4, it becomes obvious that these layers exist together in a state of mutual dependency. In real life, many holes have formed in this web. The varied elements depend on the corresponding institutions or practices at the next inner or outer layer. For instance, individual marital vows are bolstered by family faith practices, which in turn can be undergirded by home-based faith communities, which can be strengthened further yet by parishes and congregations that give a high priority to the home-based production of faith and spirituality.

Family-generated community building is thus a comprehensive approach to strengthening the settings in which children are raised. Such comprehensiveness requires participation from each of the layers: mothers and fathers, multifamily groups, representatives from schools, faith-based institutions, businesses, and local government. It requires that a community have the capacity to first assess its family institutions, their networks, and the community institutions in a thorough and complete fashion. It also entails examining how the policies that govern those institutions make them more or less amenable to engaging with families as producers.

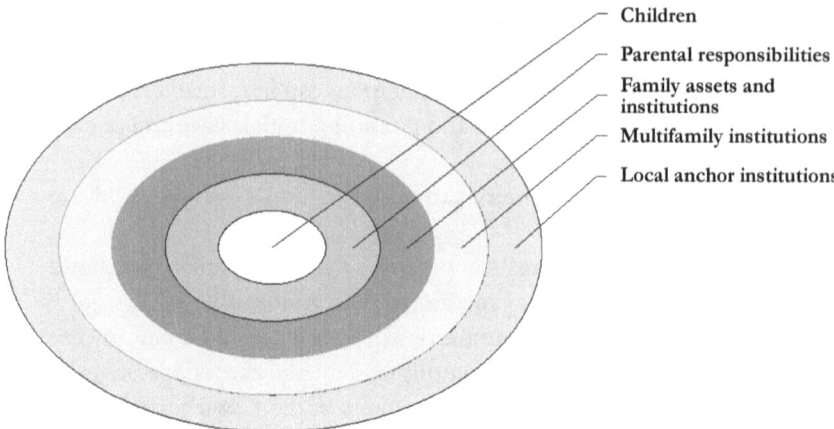

- Children
- Parental responsibilities
- Family assets and institutions
- Multifamily institutions
- Local anchor institutions

Figure 4: Layers of Local Assets and Institutions Needed by Children

Community Building When Generated by Families

Integrating the productive family into community development involves examining each stage of the process. Some emerging approaches to community development are already framed explicitly to strengthen families. The most notable efforts are the Family Economic Success and Making Connections initiative created by the Annie E. Casey Foundation. Focusing on the goal of raising the income levels of families, the Casey Foundation has supported a number of local projects.

Each of these projects, in its own way, aims to bring government, nonprofit, and neighborhood institutions together. Following the discipline of outcome-based program design, their goals are to make conditions more favorable for families to find decent jobs, make better use of income support programs (such as the Earned Income Tax Credit and Individual Development Accounts), and to use human services in ways that enhance their members' employability.

For example, one of the foundation's initiatives creates a financial skills network called Centers for Working Families. These centers provide information and counseling that help families manage their finances efficiently, build up their savings, and avoid the exploitive practices of some lenders, retailers, and mortgage companies.[46]

Some community action and assessment models already take families

---

46   See the Casey Foundation's website, www.aecf.org, for more information about the Family Economic Success and Making Connections initiatives.

into consideration, but do not make the explicit focus on thicker roles and coproduction that this book advocates. For example, the Communities That Care approach identifies a number of risk factors and protective factors around youth that determine their vulnerability to harmful social and health behaviors. Several of the factors exist at the family level.[47]

Although not presenting a community development model, Ooms recommends an ecological framework for integrating *family capital* into thinking about comprehensive community initiatives.[48] Moreover, my own previous work recommends building *family empowerment associations* through community development and policy design.[49] The point is not to denigrate the programs aimed at individuals or groups other than families. Rather, the aim is to intentionally build into the process a systematic effort to involve, study, strengthen, and evaluate the productive capacities of families.

For example, a comprehensive development process aimed at improving a community's education outcomes would still engage the formal school system heavily, but would build in, more explicitly than is usually done, various means of assessing and strengthening family capacities to coproduce education (directly, through home-based educational activity and, indirectly, through home-based development of skills and habits that facilitate learning).

Similarly, a comprehensive economic development plan would consider the same aspects of infrastructure, workforce readiness, commercial businesses, industrial firms, and other elements generally addressed through such efforts. However, family-generated community building would integrate into these considerations the explicit focus on:

- Family economic assets
- Family entrepreneurship
- Home-based businesses
- Capital sources for family enterprises
- Training infrastructure for family enterprises
- Networking and cooperatives among family enterprises
- Host settings (including incubators) for family enterprises in commercial malls or industrial parks

47   J. David Hawkins, Richard F. Catalano, Jr., and Associates, *Communities That Care* (San Francisco, CA: Jossey-Bass Publishers), 1992.

48   Theodora Ooms, *Where Is the Family in Comprehensive Community Initiatives for Children and Families?* (Washington, D.C.: Family Impact Seminar), 1996.

49   Richard S. Kordesh, *Irony and Hope in the Emerging Families Policies: A Case for Family Empowerment Associations* (University Park, PA: Institute for Policy Research and Evaluation, Pennsylvania State University), 1995.

Moreover, a comprehensive plan would examine existing plans and zoning codes for their supportiveness of home-based and other family enterprises.

Building consideration of the productive capacities of families into the community development process can produce a plan that is more directly responsive to the situations faced by children and parents today. The lack of a forthright approach to restoring the productive family is one of the major gaps in contemporary community development theory. There is a great tendency to rely on the formal institutions to do it all, or to engage families only as consumers, building thin roles for them that are subordinate to those of professionals, or avoiding such concerns as marriage and single parenthood out of a fear of antagonizing those who are sensitive about such matters.

> The lack of a forthright approach to restoring the productive family is one of the major gaps in contemporary community development. There is a great tendency to rely on the formal institutions to do it all, or to engage families only as consumers.

But when one begins with the question of how can we build the communities that children really need to thrive, there really is no route to achieving that goal without going through the task of rebuilding the family's capacities to coproduce what children need. Families must be enabled to do so in dignified partnerships with all the schools, agencies, markets, and other institutions that have over time tended to squeeze motherhood and fatherhood into the narrow, reactive—and with fathers especially—too often empty roles that they have become today.

CHAPTER 5
Critical Foundations: Habitat, Education, and Food

Three arenas of family life—the habitat, education, and food production—stand out as particularly important for family-generated community building. They also bear directly upon a family's capacity to muster power. The habitat includes the house or apartment, attached structures like balconies, garages, or sheds, plus the yard, fields, and other natural assets attached to the landscape. The habitat provides more than shelter; it can serve as a capital asset, a base to cultivate spirituality, a haven for study and reflection, a meeting place for families and friends, a space for enterprise, and a center for artistic and musical creativity.[50]

A family can more easily produce education when its habitat is designed and its spaces are arranged to facilitate study and learning. Education constitutes in its own right a critical area for family empowerment and productivity. It reaches well beyond helping children complete their lessons in school. The family also educates by cultivating positive social habits. It can impart a religious faith. It can teach marketable skills. It can convey an appreciation for democratic politics and community building.

Food production reaches into more zones of family life than just meals: it cultivates interaction with and attachment to the land, it can improve a family's budget by lessening the dependence on supermarkets and restaurants, and it can create many opportunities for learning.

These three assets interconnect like an iron triangle of family empowerment:

---

50   Richard S. Kordesh, *Creating and Sustaining Productive Family Habitats* (Oak Park, Illinois), February, 2006. (Research for this study was supported by the Annie E. Casey Foundation. Its findings do not necessarily reflect the opinions of the foundation.)

1. A decent quality habitat can enable rich and varied forms of education to take place within a family.
2. Education can increase the family's capacity to use its habitat productively.
3. Growing and preparing its own food encourages fuller use of the house and grounds. It opens up educational opportunities for adults and children.

Housing as a Productive Asset

Families who are well housed can utilize their homes in diversified ways as productive assets. Using houses productively requires an integration of functions that over time have either been separated from one another or eliminated altogether from the typical, modern home.

Integrating residential activities with commercial and industrial activities was common practice in the preindustrial towns and cities in the United States. Although not as widespread after the nineteenth century, one could still find in dense, urban neighborhoods many examples of family-run shops where the families lived in apartments above or behind their commercial spaces.

The built environment matters: thicker roles for mothers and fathers can be aided by housing design that blends different functions into more general-use spaces.

It is a natural thing for a family to combine its work and residential activities. It makes life easier: long commutes to work are unnecessary, children are more easily monitored, teenagers find their first jobs working in the family shop, and many relationships with neighbors form as they frequent one another's premises.

Many examples like this one still exist in older cities: A neighborhood store still sells groceries in an inner-ring Chicago suburb. Built in the early twentieth century, the property has long housed a family enterprise, with the families changing as the ethnic makeup of the neighborhood evolved. In the 1960s and '70s, it was owned by an Italian family and today, Latinos.

Such stores can sometimes allow local families to purchase groceries on credit. These can become personal places—the owners know their customers. They know who is working; who can be trusted with credit; and what kind of meats, vegetables, or pastries their neighbor-customers prefer.

A small family store creates a hub for social interaction. Neighborhood news can travel quickly; the proprietors have time to talk with their customers. Children can walk to such shops on errands for their parents or to make their own purchases. The children of the owners and the customers might attend the same school.

Such establishments are possible in part because of the way they spatially integrate the business and residential functions of the shop owners. A bell on the door might ring when a customer enters the store. One of the family members hears it from the back of the store—where the kitchen might be adjacent to the shop's storeroom—and knows that a customer is waiting. One can tend to a soup or casserole for the family dinner and wait on customers as well.

Many potentially productive spaces exist in homes, even though in the case of modern houses, they were not necessarily designed that way. Many bedrooms have been converted into home offices. Newer home designs intentionally demarcate spaces for offices.

Mixed-use spaces can be created as homes are remodeled. Children's separate bedrooms can be joined for central computer spaces and small libraries, preserving privacy with partitions, but turning rooms essentially designed for sleeping and storing clothes into productive educational centers as well.

While many homes are retrofitted to include workspace, others are designed intentionally as live/work spaces. Live/work design is achieving more influence due to the Internet and as a result of the growing costs of commuting. Live/work design makes for general-use spaces that can be adapted for studios, workshops, or mixed living and working functions. It might build in thicker walls, soundproofing, or higher capacity electrical wiring. Some live/work spaces are emerging in multiple unit structures in which the work spaces are shared by residents from different apartments or condominiums. Some zoning ordinances are being updated to define the parameters for live/work buildings where residents will engage in light industrial activity (necessitating ventilation and space for shipping, for example).[51]

Consider the many productive activities that are enabled by computers: photographic production, music composition, writing, publishing, and the creation of family websites. Why not create spaces in homes where such productivity is made easier? Small businesses can emerge from such activities. Educational exercises can be supported.

Certain kinds of microenterprises in homes are indeed increasing. Some funders and community development organizations focus on them as core antipoverty tools. The types of goods that home-based enterprises create stretch endlessly: pottery, jewelry, specialty foods, crafts of many kinds, and other items.

A new body of literature has emerged in recent years that recaptures from the momentum toward out-of-home work some of the energy needed to sustain in-home work. New categories of careers—"virtual assistants,"

---

51   A good source on the Internet, created by architect Tom Dolan, is www.live-work.com/lwi.

for example—are explicitly defined by their in-home status. Advocates of home-based enterprises intentionally tie these forms of work to the social and cultural interests of families that are partly grounded and expressed by uses of their habitats. While much of this effort seems to be driven by mothers, growing numbers of fathers have also entered the quest to reconnect home, family, and work.[52]

With the intentional and creative use of space, a home can also serve as a spiritual sanctuary. Religious paintings, symbols, and books can be placed throughout the house. Some families establish particular rooms as spiritual centers complete with altars. Is this a new or old idea? For Christians, it was new 2000 years ago when they were growing their faith on the margins of Roman power. They prayed in homes because they feared persecution. But it also makes sense for family life in times when faith is protected by the state: it is a natural act to integrate worship and residence.

Integrating functions enables integration of roles as parent, business owner, and spiritual mentor. The integration of mothers' and fathers' roles thickens them. Through their work, rather than after they leave their work roles, they teach their children. Through their teaching, parents guide their children's behavior. Mothers and fathers then make them ready to succeed in school. Through activities in their home-based shops, they make their neighborhoods more hospitable for other families. Community emerges as a by-product of thick, productive family roles.

Education

In order for education to "begin at the home," as the adage goes, there must be a home to begin with. It does not have to be a place that the parents own, but a home it must nevertheless be. Housing provides a framework for this next essential productive function: education. However, housing is only part of the foundation beneath this important area of activity.

Although the education literature does not usually phrase it this way, education must be coproduced by mothers, fathers, and professionals. Schools have assumed so much power—and parents have been diverted so much from their roles by their employers—that what is usually recommended as parent involvement makes parents into adjuncts to the professionals.

52   See for example, Tory Johnson and Robyn Freedman Spizman, *Will Work from Home* (New York: Berkeley Books), 2008; Christine Durst and Michael Haaren, *The 2-Second Commute* (Franklin Lakes, NJ: Career Press), 2005; Paul Edwards and Sarah Edwards, *Working from Home: Everything You Need to Know about Living and Working under the Same Roof* (Los Angeles, CA: Jeremy P. Tarcher, Inc.),1985; and Paul Edwards and Sarah Edwards, *The Best Home Businesses for People 50+* (New York: Jeremy P. Tarcher/Penguin), 2004.

Whether public schools displace parents from their rightful educational roles or enable them to find stronger roles has long been a contentious issue in education policy. Some analysts criticize the formal education system as fundamentally hostile to families and communities.

John Taylor Gatto, an accomplished teacher in the public schools for twenty-seven years, left his tenured position in order to change them. He argues that schools have become routinized, standardized, and boring. According to Gatto, a principal failing of the public school system arises from the way it cut the family out of its rightful educational role.

As a critic of the position that schools must expand in order to compensate for the family's decline, he holds that building more programs into schools before and after regular classes does not level the playing field between children with strong families and those with weak families.[53]

As Gatto sees it, expanding schools in order to fill the gaps left by weak families ironically disguises the schools' own complicity in weakening the family. More programs in schools, even when they involve parents in preset roles, deter the family from using the time to make itself stronger. Then, with further irony, families are blamed by educators for, in effect, not being families.[54]

Is it really parent empowerment when the roles that parents play in education are constructed completely by teachers?

Gatto advocates a complete reconstruction of education that would decertify teachers and would emphasize community service, highly diversified educational settings, and a restoration of the family's and community's time for educating children.

The growth of homeschooling in the United States shows that many families agree with Gatto and other critics of public education. Homeschooling parents reverse the trend toward expanding school functions. They retake their educational roles and make their own homes into schools. Some create their own curricula. Others utilize curricula available for purchase.[55]

Interestingly, some of the curricula that parents can purchase through the Internet offer the option of teaching advisory services. Certified teachers can be consulted by parents when they get stuck on particular math or science problems. Turning the typical situation on its head, in which a parent might serve as a classroom aide to a teacher in a formal school, the professional teacher works as an aide at the discretion of the parent.

Of course, many proponents of public education argue that schools can be

---

53   John Taylor Gatto, *Dumbing Us Down: The Hidden Curriculum of Compulsory Schooling* (Gabriola Island, B.C.: New Society Publishers), 1992, 74.

54   Ibid., 74.

55   For example, see the Calvert School, www.Calvert.com, and The Trent Academy, www.theschools.com.

organized so that new, enriching educational roles can be created for parents that would not be possible without such institutions. One highly regarded advocate of this view is James Comer, whose School Development Program has been widely embraced. As he sees it, the home, along with society, the school, and other social networks must operate in harmony if all of the child's "developmental pathways" (physical, psychological, social, cognitive, ethical, and linguistic) are to be addressed.

Poor children, in particular, need a school with a social development program in place in order to overcome the deprivations of poverty:

> A child from a poor, marginal family is likely to enter school without adequate preparation. The child may arrive without ever having learned such social skills as negotiation and compromise. A child who is expected to read at school may come from a home where no one reads and where no parent ever read a bedtime story. It is because such circumstances are at variance with mainstream expectations that these children are often considered aggressive or "bad" and often judged to be of low academic potential.[56]

Schools, in fact, vary in how deeply they embrace parents as coeducators. Parents vary in how enthusiastically they seek to play such productive teaching roles. Clearly, poor and illiterate parents themselves need help if they are to become capable of acting as coeducators. But, as was pointed out earlier, many are poor because in other realms, especially in the economy, they and previous generations were displaced from the productive economic roles that would have helped to prevent their impoverishment. Thus, in order to become adept in their roles as coeducators, they also need empowerment in the economic and cultural uses of their habitats.

Nevertheless, if one considers education holistically, it is easy to identify many components of thick, coproducer roles that children need their parents to take. Important dimensions of such roles include the following.

- Teaching children the various aspects of personal hygiene and preventive health practices.
- Teaching children moral and ethical rules of behavior.
- Teaching children how to read.
- Teaching children how to count and manipulate numbers.
- Teaching children a spoken language.

---

56   James P. Comer, Norris M. Haynes, Edward T. Joyner, and Michael Ben-Avie, *Rallying the Whole Village: The Comer Process for Reforming Education* (New York: Teachers College, Columbia University), 1996, 16.

- Teaching children about the family's religious tradition.
- Teaching children how to interpret television programming and movies from a moral perspective.
- Teaching children basic coordination and fitness skills, as well as more refined skills in sports such as baseball or basketball.
- Teaching children how to get along or how to defend themselves when bullied.

These are all elements of the teaching roles that children need for their parents to take. At a very minimum, the above skills and guidelines for acting out values must be coproduced by parents and teachers. In truth, children generally do best when their parents are their first teachers of these and other lessons.

The coproduction of education is a foundational role in family-generated community building because it is so holistic: it affects the child's inner development, social development, and his or her understanding of the larger world.

Education, as Thomas Jefferson recognized, is fundamentally important to building a healthy democracy. He and the Framers assumed the family's presence; it would complement the public schooling that he advocated. Universal education in his view would have been embedded within communities, clusters of farms, and small family institutions.

The explosive growth of homeschooling today demonstrates that many parents have decided to thicken their educational roles by turning their own homes into miniature schools. Perhaps this movement will create enough urgency in the educational field that homes can be valued as schools unto themselves, rather than as extensions of the school's program.

Such a view would not by any means require that children be schooled exclusively at home, as more are every year. Rather, a co-schooling model could support the parents' roles, strengthen the capacities of parents who themselves need some basic education, and reorient the perspectives of professional teachers toward the other "schools" that their children attend in their homes.

Some popular approaches to parent education in the early childhood field have begun to move in this direction. Working from family resource centers, which are often located in schools, "family visitors," many of whom are themselves parents, go into homes to teach new parents the various benchmarks of healthy child development.[57] They teach nutritional lessons, family management skills, nonabusive disciplinary techniques, and many

---

57   Parents as Teachers is one of the first organizations to develop this approach. For more information, go to www.Parentsasteachers.org.

other skills. Let this effort be a beginning in the rebalancing of power between the formal school and the home as a place for delivering education.

Food

Building a healthy relationship between families and the land on which they live is an important feature of family-generated community building. The capacity to produce at least some of its own food, as well as food for other families and community members, is one of the most neglected capacities. To a large extent, except for families in rural areas, food production is considered as an insignificant, irrelevant form of empowerment.

Yet, for poor and middle-class families, there are rewarding opportunities for producing food for one's own family. It does not require much space. Nor does it call for a large capital investment. It is mostly a matter of becoming intentional about it, taking the time, and creating the space.

In a small, urban garden space, many vegetables can be grown vertically. These include cucumbers, eggplants, beans, tomatoes, zucchini, and various types of squash.

Due to the exploding number of teaching and technological resources available, it is possible to grow many pounds of vegetables and fruits on modest-sized urban properties. With the use of hoop houses and hydroponics, it is also feasible to grow food year-round in cold climates. Techniques for square-foot gardening can be learned, making maximum productive use of small, raised beds. With the use of rain barrels, water can be captured and kept clean for use in dry climates, or during dry spells elsewhere.

Composting year-round provides an internal process for keeping the gardens well fertilized. More cool storage, such as earth-berm sheds, are being constructed in family habitats. Solar energy is being used by an increasing number of sustainable farms, large and small, to power irrigation systems, including those in small, hydroponic gardens.

Good sources on home-based gardening exist on the Internet as well as in book form. Classes for home-based food production are offered at community colleges and nonprofit organizations that promote urban farming or food production in small growing spaces.[58]

Some communities have created resource centers, networks, and associations whose mission is to foster community and home-based food production. The Urban Harvest organization in Houston, Texas, has created

---

58   An inspiring and extremely informative source on the web is www.pathtofree dom.com.

a designated space for home-based gardeners and their produce at its larger, regional farmers' market.[59]

At a scale that seems achievable with the right approach to organizing, home-based food production could transform a community. Imagine what could result from a modest, yet determined effort to create an eight-foot by eight-foot raised bed in every family property in a neighborhood. In the case of multiple-unit buildings, gardening could be done in designated shared spaces. Vegetables could be grown in containers on decks and roofs. Families could tend productive plots together in community gardens. In fact, many already do.[60]

Consider the many health benefits that would arise from a commitment to growing food at home. Obesity would diminish: families would not be drawn so easily to fast-food establishments. Obesity raises the probability of many health maladies, including diabetes, strokes, heart attacks, joint problems, and hypertension.

Consider as well the benefits to the family budget. Homegrown food is cheaper than food at the supermarket. It is certainly less expensive than what one buys in a restaurant.

Imagine the impact on low-income neighborhoods where supermarkets are in short supply, and empty yet tillable lots are plentiful. Some such efforts in urban farming are underway.

Families also benefit as social units from productive gardening. They work together—seeding, tending, weeding, watering, pruning, fertilizing, and harvesting.

They learn together about climate, soil quality, bugs, pests, plant disease, the stages of plant growth, the use and conservation of water, and other matters complementary to the botany, biology, chemistry, environmental science, and earth science that the children will study in school. Children who garden come to school with a working knowledge of such subjects. Mothers' and fathers' roles thicken as they mentor their children in the garden.

Communities benefit when many families and residents are working the land. People become reacquainted with the places they inhabit. They begin to know them from the ground up. They recognize how water flows and where it collects when it rains. Capturing rainwater for use in the garden becomes a routine concern. Gardeners grow in attentiveness to the presence of pollutants. They become more vigilant and dedicated to their places.

Places that exhibit such vigilance and productivity raise the comfort level of potential outside investors and government leaders. Banks and

59   See www.urbanharvest.org.

60   Go to links to community gardening websites at the Blue House Institute's website: www.bluehouseinstitute.com/gardening.

businesses look at places that are well cared for by their inhabitants as better investment risks than places where neglect and exploitation of the land have been the norm. It is not only that the land is more costly to rehabilitate; the community's sense of responsibility is not as evident.

With responsible business investments, capital becomes easier to acquire for other enterprises. Unproductive land becomes productive. The increased vitality attracts more capital. More vitality increases stability; the vigilance about the quality of the land helps ensure that new economic activities adhere to sustainability. From the ground under the feet of inhabitants arises the energy for family-generated community building.

CHAPTER 6
Building Community around Children

Productive family institutions and thick roles for mothers and fathers are essential elements of family-generated community building. But what is *community* itself? When does building family institutions actually contribute to the formation of a community? How does building a thicker role for a mother or father ensure that a stronger community emerges around children?

Community itself is a challenging notion and deserves its own examination. One could imagine much of the institution building, network creation, coproduction, and family agriculture taking place without a community ever forming among those entities. What else, beyond institution building, must take place?

Let us begin with a definition: *community* exists among people when they share values, visions of their future, stories of their local history, and affection for the places where they live and work.[61] Therefore, entities like cities or neighborhoods are not always communities. Some are too divided internally to be communities.

Communities that practice democratic decision making are best able to develop healthy civic traits in their children and adult members.

In such places, children learn to trust others, and they learn positive social habits that help them contribute to the well-being of others. Families must be able to exercise productive capacities in the social, civic, economic, and religio-cultural realms in order to participate in building and sustaining community. Unfortunately, many forces are at work in our culture and political economy that undermine community. On the positive side, many resources can be mobilized to restore it.

---

61   Richard Kordesh, "Community for Children," (*National Civic Review*, Fall 1991), 374–380.

Elements of Community

Let us expand upon each of the above statements.

Communities establish their unique identities in part by holding in common, and practicing, particular values. For example, some communities become known for creating mutually respectful relations among diverse ethnic and racial groups. Others identify deeply with the unique traditions in their ethnic heritage. Consider, for example, the many ways in which Mexican communities draw on the symbol of the Virgin of Guadalupe to keep alive their traditions and values. She represents many things at once: religious faith, the sanctity of the family, and even resistance to political oppression. Her image on murals, in religious festivals, in statues, and in many other manifestations can be seen throughout a Mexican neighborhood.

A community might be recognized for the high quality of its athletic programs—not only how many championships they win, but also the standards of excellence in training, performance, and community relations that they manage to maintain through a community-wide commitment. Or an empowering value might be placed on a particular musical form, such as the blues or gospel in some African-American neighborhoods. Whether it is sports, music, or social practices, community is generated when its people participate together in honoring and reinforcing the shared values that they hold.

Community is more likely to be present when people know collectively where they want to be in the future. Community planning, therefore, which is broadly participatory, is a necessary element of building community. The visions that arise from planning can vary from one place to the next, depending in part on the values, but also on the problems and opportunities that the people face. One community might be strengthened by its pursuit of an inspiring, sustainable growth policy. Another might be galvanized by its goals for an excellent education system. A rural community might be inspired by its goals for a diversified, robust mix of small farms and thriving enterprises.

Communities also need shared stories or myths[62] that inspire and embolden their members. One place might find courage in a story about how its ancestors recovered from a fire or natural disaster. Stories about the flood from which the city recovered or the tornado from which a neighborhood

---

62   This usage of myth does not refer to something that isn't true, but rather to its true meaning of legendary stories that inspire faith and exhort us to face challenges.

rebuilt help people rally together. A healthy myth might arise over the decades about an athletic team that exceeded its potential and won a championship. There might be stories of leaders who founded the community or who resolved a crisis that helped its people and institutions move forward. For example, efforts to rebuild New Orleans after Hurricane Katrina depend in part on the abilities of leaders to construct inspiring, public myths that invoke resilience, tenacity, and heroism. Museums, festivals, libraries, murals, statues, and dedicated landmarks help solidify the power of such myths so that generations can relive them and even add to them.

Place matters in family-generated community building. Attachment to a geographical area provides a rich concentration of material for fostering productive family institutions and for building the healthy ecology around children. It must be recognized as a critical element of community. A relationship to a small place is obviously important to younger children; parents often define the boundaries of their neighborhoods by how far their children go from home in order to play. Parents often want their toddlers to wander no farther than the point where they can be seen from the front steps. It is more common for school-aged children to cross residential streets in order to play with friends. Teens need shared places that they can help shape and in which they can grow. In fact, one of the factors that contributes to problems in adolescence is their potential estrangement from the community. Access to cars and long trips to their distant high schools detach them from the places where they grew up, encouraging them to become a group separate from the community.

Amenities of place that can be drawn upon to build community include parks, gardens, rivers, streams, forestland, and wildlife habitats. The natural landscape of a place—a significant hill, a point on

Personal Illustration:
I coached youth baseball teams on which my sons played for nine years. One of the challenges in coaching is helping the kids "hold it together" when they are losing or when a couple of kids whose skills are not that advanced make errors in critical situations. It's important to not let the pushier boys bully or scapegoat those who've made mistakes. I look for "teaching moments" when there isn't a tense situation at hand to help forestall scapegoating. For instance, practicing good communication on the field keeps everyone talking positively. I emphasize, as do most good coaches, the importance of building the teammates' confidence and letting coaches do the criticism. You somehow mention this and practice it every day. I do believe that such practices spill over into school and eventually civic behavior. Trust and team building learned in baseball are good for citizenship and democratic community building.

a lake, or a bend in a river—gives people features that add to a community's identity. Many cities and towns are even named after significant features of their landscapes.

The fruits of a place can nourish community as well. Rural communities become stronger when they organize efforts to buy locally produced vegetables, fruit, and grains. Festivals and farmers' markets are organized around locally grown produce as well as local crafts.

Urban settings also derive their identities as communities from things built by people. How many neighborhoods are named after fountains, squares, monuments, and historical landmarks?

Communities are able to cultivate positive civic habits in children as they create many forums for democratic decision making. Children learn how to solve problems through dialogue, listening, considering facts dispassionately, weighing diverse points of view, and coming to reasonable compromises when they see adults around them behaving similarly. Communities that make democracy common practice in their politics, social institutions, and even in families, ensure that children will learn democracy by living it.

A requisite of democratic participation is a sufficient amount of trust among members for one another. Childhood is a critically important time to learn to trust others. The renowned psychologist Erik Erikson held that learning to trust others was one of the first necessary milestones that a young child had to achieve in order to then master others.[63] The others include the capacity to form a positive personal identity, a sense of competence, and eventually, *generativity*—being able as an adult to devote oneself in part to working on behalf of the next generation. At this stage of development, the person shifts his or her goals to emphasize a positive impact on the communities in which children will be growing up in the future. These goals could include protecting the environment, setting up a stable financial future for them, or educating them today so that they can form families successfully and govern communities effectively. Community enables adults to reach this stage at which striving for such goals becomes an imperative of personal fulfillment.

As the adage goes, "Children learn what they live."

---

63   Erik H. Erikson, op. cit., 1963. For an eloquent discussion of "generativity" see Bellah et al., *Habits of the Heart: Individualism and Commitment in American Life* (London: University of California Press), 1985.

Families Must Cultivate the Capacity to Trust

The capacity to build a strong family depends on generativity, which in turn depends on being able to trust. The family is the first place where a child will either learn to trust others or not. A child's capacity to trust others can be shattered by broken promises, failed vows, the disappearance of a mother or father, or the failure of the family, community, or society to provide such basic necessities as food, shelter, safety, or care in an emergency.[64]

In a more extreme but still too common case, homelessness can destroy a child's trust in others. So can routine hunger, unchecked neighborhood violence, exposure to war, and child abuse.[65]

Building trust in a child is a task for thick motherhood and fatherhood. Productive roles and institutions bolster thick parent roles. Predictability matters. Building trust requires time, teaching, and follow-through. It requires being present to a child.

It is easier to create and maintain thick roles in a family when productive activities are part of the routine: gardening, building things in a workshop, running a business from home, teaching at home, preparing and eating meals, as well as praying together. Trust and other positive social habits are necessary for participation in a democracy—they are among the goods that a family can coproduce with others in a strong community.

An untold number of lessons can be learned from watching and participating in the planting and tending of a garden. Much teaching can take place when a mother or father coaches a baseball or soccer team. These are thick tasks. Communities need for parents to be carrying them out, and strong communities are required to support them. To carry through the ecological theme: healthy communities create good habitats for productive families.

Forces That Stifle Community

Forces that seem endemic to our political culture, economic system, and institutional power arrangements can make it very difficult to build community around children. These tensions—even contradictions—in our society have long been the concern of thoughtful social and political analysts. Alexis de Tocqueville's great work, *Democracy in America*, marveled at the spirit of volunteerism that was flourishing in the United States, but warned that the freedom that enabled it might devolve into a destructive kind of selfishness,

---

64   Judith S. Wallerstein, Julia M. Lewis, and Sandra Blakeslee, *The Unexpected Legacy of Divorce* (New York: Hyperion), 2000.

65   James Garbarino, Nancy Dubrow, Kathleen Kostelny, and Carole Pardo, *Children in Danger* (San Francisco, CA: Jossey-Bass Publishers), 1992.

or egoism.[66] Writers in the Progressive era concerned themselves with the destructive impacts of concentrated economic power on community.

More recently, communitarian writers, most notably Amitai Etzioni, have argued that an emphasis in our society on rights versus responsibilities tips the balance against community.[67] Religious scholars from various backgrounds have long warned that an overemphasis on individualism, as well as complacency about inequality, threaten the foundations of community in the United States. There are specific threats to each of the elements of community identified above. Knowing them can help counter them.

A community's capacity to embrace common values can be threatened by an exclusive preoccupation with freedom or diversity. A reticence to identify common values might stem from a historical lack of trust among different ethnic or racial groups. In such a case, it might be easier in the short term to put on the face of a pseudo-community or to ignore its absence by focusing on the benefits of diversity. Diversity is a healthy thing, but it does not on its own signal the presence of community. Ironically, in the absence of real common ground, diversity might be the only value on which people agree.

A locality might be unable to agree on common values when some groups dominate others. If there are particular neighborhoods, business elites, religious denominations, political cliques, ethnic enclaves, or racial groups that hold the dominant position in a community, they will impose their values upon it. Under such conditions, unless there is open conflict over power, it might appear on the surface that the locality is stable and enjoys a consensus on values.

Or it might be the case that the dominant group has been able to wall itself off from the others and behave, in effect, as a separate community. It might use political tools such as municipal incorporation or exclusionary zoning to protect its exclusivity. Community remains fractured as a result.

A locality might be too internally divided or badly led to agree on goals that inspire consensus. Even when there might be an agreement on common values, the government might be too institutionally fragmented to establish a consensus on comprehensive plans. The political institutions might not enjoy enough legitimacy among the citizens, and thereby they might not be able to engage them in planning.

---

66   Alexis de Tocqueville, *Democracy in America* (New York: Mentor Books), 1956.
67   Amitai Etzioni, *The Spirit of Community* (New York: Crown Publishers), 1993.

The local political culture might be so deeply adversarial that residents and leaders have not learned how to plan together. Competition among varied "fiefdoms" and power centers might be a way of life; those who have gained power from that way of life will not be enthusiastic about giving it up. Journalists might find more career incentives in fostering conflict and antipathy than cooperation and community building. Television media might thrive commercially on stories that highlight the failures and foibles of men and women in politics. Cynicism about the possibility of community might be so deeply ingrained that, perversely, it remains the only fuel to energize political conversation.

Localities might be prevented by historical antagonisms from agreeing on shared myths or stories. To some, statues of, busts of, and stories about, the traditional "town fathers" might be inspiring; to others they might represent continuing evidence of local racism or sexism. One ethnic group's hero might be another group's villain. Groups that view themselves as historically oppressed within a particular locality might thrive on myths of heroes who have stood up against the other more-dominant groups and won particular rights. The internal solidarity of groups formed in response to oppression might depend, even if their oppression ends, on continuing to nurse long-standing grievances that persist in fracturing the larger community.

Localities might be so fragmented geographically by planning and zoning decisions that they are not able to solidify their sense of place. New roads, especially interstate highways, have cut through many previously cohesive neighborhoods. Many suburban areas are zoned to so isolate commercial, residential, and spaces for public use that they have in effect zoned away the sense of place. "New urbanist" critics of such practices are right: taking the walkability out of the community diminishes a sense of place. When residents have to drive their cars to schools, to shopping centers, to recreation facilities, and even to the homes of their children's friends, transportation becomes a means of stifling, rather than supporting, a sense of place.

Localities might be too damaged environmentally to support a healthy sense of place. There are older, industrial areas in some cities where poor people still live that are simply too filled with health risks and industrial waste to sustain vitality. There are areas that have been mined so heavily that the land is too scarred for community development. In some places, overfarming, overgrazing, or overbuilding have diluted the water supplies and stripped the land bare of fertile topsoil. Streams or rivers that once had served as the attraction for building settlements might be too polluted to serve as a healthy source of drinking water.

Overcoming the Forces That Stifle Community

Building good communities around children will require actions on the part of parents, community leaders, planners, policy makers, and citizens in general.

- **Parents will need to work together to ground their lives more in their neighborhoods and communities.** The thicker roles addressed above will be necessary to better defend their family boundaries, including their marital commitments. They will need to organize their lives as best as they are able to function as coproducers with local institutions of such good things as education, housing, positive moral development, and food.

- **People who inhabit and work in shared places will need to draw on their common grounds—the earth under their feet—as a source of community building.** No matter what their differences might be as people, no matter how their political system might divide them, and no matter what grievances they might hold against one another, the place on which they live is one place. It will be healthier for them if they care for it, and it will provide them with many natural amenities upon which to find shared concerns, symbols, stories, and goals.

- **Political leaders, media organizations, and citizens will need to take more seriously the need to counterbalance the adversarial and cynical tendencies in the political culture with efforts to build consensus and trust.** Personal attacks on the character of others, one-upping opponents with cutting one-line criticisms, labeling, and verbal knee-capping seem so endemic to electoral politics that it might be difficult to imagine another way. But that is a sign of how serious is the need to renew the communitarian energies in the political culture. And they are there. Leaders are still capable of arguing policy differences without seeking to personally humiliate opponents. There are newspaper writers and television reporters who are quite good at getting to the truth without playing on public cynicism to garner attention. There is a wealth of literature, contemporary and historical, that can inform such a renewal.[68]

- **Policies will need to redress the injustices that make it extremely difficult for some groups, especially African-Americans and Native Americans, to engage successfully in family-generated community building.** Place-based community development strategies in particular will be helpful in enabling parents and leaders in our most distressed communities to do what it takes to build their own productive institutions, to become coproducers of what their children need, to create dignified roles for fathers to take, and to participate proactively in planning and policy development. The tools, the institutions, and strategies are within reach. Consensus building and leadership can make them work toward these ends.

Children need to see that the adults who have brought them into this world know how to take care of them. They need to see that the adults know how to work together to make their places safe, clean, and beautiful. They need to learn that it is possible to trust others to keep their promises.

Children learn of community from their own experiences with it. Family-generated community building will help them become good mothers, fathers, and community builders themselves.

---

68   A good entry point into this literature is *The National Civic Review*, a journal published by the National Civic League, Denver, Colorado.

CHAPTER 7

Integrating the Productive Family into Community Problem Solving

We have approached the subject of how to strengthen productive families and engage them in community building through several angles. Chapter three addressed steps for creating thicker parent roles. Chapter four considered the stages of community building. Chapter five delved into the means for building up enterprises and other productive activities in the family's habitat. This chapter and the next unpack in more depth how to involve families productively in the community building process. We begin with family engagement in the day-to-day problem solving that takes place in localities.

In order to illustrate more fully how to make the productive family a more central concern in community development, this chapter presents a series of questions. The questions are organized around the typical stages of community problem solving: setting the stage for the community decision-making process, defining the community's problems, setting goals and strategies, and evaluating outcomes. The questions highlight the significance that the community can attribute to the productive family.

Community problem solving is always taking place. It might be addressing school issues, crime prevention, housing, business development, health, or other matters. This is usually the way that community development proceeds:

1. A problem emerges.
2. It becomes recognized as a significant local issue.
3. A task force or committee is formed representing varied interests.

4. Facts are gathered.
5. Options are weighed.
6. Hearings might be held.
7. An action plan with goals and timetables emerges.
8. Some means of measuring success or failure is identified.

The questions posed below constitute an "audit guide" that addresses a community's readiness to solve its problems using the tenets of family-generated community building. They illustrate what community problem solving could look like were the productive family and its institutions integrated intentionally into the local decision-making routines.

Preparations

First, we must consider how a task force or community development committee initially organizes itself, sets parameters on what issues it will consider relevant, how open its agenda will be, and how broad a range of alternative actions will be deemed legitimate. The following questions address this preliminary phase—even before a group analyzes in any depth the problem that prompted its formation.

- **Has the situation been framed in a way that attributes appropriate significance to the productive family?** For example, if the issue has to do with elementary education, does the group's mission statement or the committee's charge contain language recognizing that families and schools together produce learning? Or are there signs in any preliminary documents (staff memos, minutes from school board meetings, orientation papers) that families and parents are only going to be blamed for problematic results in school performance?

- **Does the process for selecting the major players include mothers, fathers, and other advocates for productive families?** In particular, are there going to be parents on the decision-making group who are already strong producers of learning? Are homeschooling parents included? If the issue has to do with developing housing, are mothers and fathers who are seeking housing, especially for its productive uses, going to be invited proactively to participate? Are organizations known for taking aggressive actions on behalf of productive families built into the process?

- **Does the orientation provided by lead staff address itself to the schedules and perspectives of productive families?** At the beginning of a task force's tenure, there is usually an orientation—a training session that provides background information on the issue at stake, the purpose and timetable of the planning project, an introduction to members and staff, and other important preliminary information. Planners or school professionals can often exercise considerable influence over task forces, beginning with the orientations that they deliver. Consider, for example, the importance of the project's logistics. Scheduling must take into account the unique time demands faced by families with children. For example, don't allow meetings to run late into the evening. Hold workshops on Saturday afternoons when older children or spouses can take care of the children while one parent is participating in a meeting. Find some parent volunteers to watch the children in a school classroom or playroom while committees meet in another section of the building.

- **Does the orientation make clear that the agenda is open to solutions involving coproduction between families and community institutions?** If it is an education issue, does the orientation signal that bolstering the family's capacity to teach is as important as the school's capacity to teach? Does it suggest that education is seen as something that families and schools produce together? In the case of an economic development issue, is sufficient recognition given in the orientation to the productive potential of family enterprises—home-based and otherwise?

- **Does the host organization's history suggest that it will engage respectfully with productive families and their institutions?** Hosting a task force or committee might mean something as perfunctory as providing meeting space. How welcoming has it been in the past to parents as equal participants with professionals? Or it might include more influential tasks such as loaning staff members, providing the group's planning budget, paying for trips, or other significant contributions. Consider the instance of a group being formed to address a high rate of mortgage foreclosures and a lack of affordable housing in a neighborhood. If the host is a major bank, one needs to know, from the standpoint of family-generated community building, how proactive a stance that bank has taken historically toward families who are having trouble making their mortgage payments. Has it shown a willingness to work with families as partners in renegotiating their financing? Or if a city's planning department is hosting the group, has it acted aggressively in the past to press developers to build enough modestly priced units for families?

Defining the Problem

How a community group defines a problem sets parameters around the range of solutions that will be open for consideration. Some groups spend much time and effort to develop data, consult research, acquire testimony from experts, and hold debates before they arrive at a problem statement. Others proceed less rationally, and almost take the problem definition as given. One often hears comments such as, "We already know what's wrong; we just need to get on with fixing it." Such statements might reflect a natural impatience to act, but they might be a strategic effort to limit the agenda.

- **Has the discussion of the problem in the community used information that highlights the importance of productive families, their assets, and institutions?** How a task force defines a problem is often affected by the way newspaper stories or political events previously defined it. Will the staff or task force members make sure that information bearing on the productive capacities of families will be considered, whether or not it had been presented during earlier discussions in the community?

- **Did the events that made the problem a "burning issue" locally bias the problem definition for or against productive family institutions?** It might be that poor results in a school's standardized test scores made the issue visible enough to become the focus of a new task force. However, perhaps the poor scores were discussed exclusively as a matter to be solved by introducing changes into the school or classroom. Although such matters are important, they are not the only considerations. Perhaps literacy education for parents would make them better teachers of reading, and thus eventually improve test scores. Perhaps some parents could be recruited as tutors, or contracted to offer reading workshops in their homes.

- **Does the presentation of the problem consider factually the readiness of community institutions to work respectfully with productive families and their institutions?** For example, if the deterioration of an important commercial block is a focus, does the definition of the problem consider the fact that some lenders or city agencies might preclude in their lending criteria giving support to small or new family enterprises? Are family enterprises among the types of businesses considered at the outset as targets for revitalization funding? Similarly, if poor school outcomes are a concern, does the problem definition consider the possibility that a lack of readiness on the part of the school or the district to work respectfully with families is a factor?

- **Has the problem been framed in a way that recognizes the importance of the productive family?** Generally speaking, no matter what the issue, problems emerge in communities in part because families have not been able to prevent them. They might not have possessed the productive resources and institutions necessary to produce the goods that would have helped to prevent their emergence. For example, if the problem has to do with neighborhood crime, families living in the target area can organize individually and through networks to put more "eyes on the streets." Have they? Do they have organized routines for reporting suspicious activity? Can they monitor one another's homes? Safety is a good that families help produce: does the problem definition embraced by the task force recognize that a gap in the families' capacities to produce it helps explain the occurrence of crime?

Setting Goals and Determining Strategies

After a group has agreed on the problem and its causes, it deliberates on what goals it wants to pursue and on actions it would take to achieve the goals. This is another stage of community problem solving in which the battle can be won or lost for the productive family and its institutions.

- **Is there a working *theory of change* guiding the group's selection of goals and strategies? If so, does it see families helping to produce the changes needed to achieve the goals?** Suppose that a task force decides that a way to prevent the occurrence of Type II diabetes in its adult population is to lower the obesity rate, and to do that it must improve residents' diets. Does the theory of change implied in this vision recognize that one important step to improving diets is to help families grow vegetables and fruits organically in their own gardens? Or, if a planning group decides that one of the ways to encourage job creation is to foster small business development at the neighborhood level, does it consider in its vision for change providing support for families who want to build suitable spaces into their homes for small businesses? The task force will consider such steps when it has been sufficiently oriented to the productive capacities of families.

- **Do the goals and strategies specify how productive assets and institutions of families must be stronger in order to prevent the problem's future occurrence?** The more intentional and specific the action steps, the better. For example, a plan to increase the production of vegetables by families would be easier to achieve with very specific objectives addressing how low-income families could acquire tools, how purchasing pools could be set up to make soil and mulch affordable, how to provide training in pest and disease management, and other fine points of gardening. In the case of home businesses, a plan could specify in its objectives what loan pools would be established to make low-interest financing available, what training could be provided to families in managing small businesses at home, what bulk software purchases could help family business owners track their finances, and other detailed aspects of small business formation.

- **Do the statements of goals and strategies specify how networks among productive family institutions will be strengthened?** Not only must individual family institutions be strengthened, they must also be formed into resilient networks. These networks must become part of the community's productive infrastructure in education, health, and economic development. For example, networks among families in the same housing development help them distribute and share food from the individual gardens. Or, they can help organize common family gardens. Family educational networks can help parents support one another in their teaching roles. They can share books purchased privately, expanding collectively the library of resources available to adults and children. Imagine if thirty families had libraries of thirty books each; collectively that would add up to nine hundred books potentially available to share. But such sharing takes intentional organizing, and community development can energize such network formation.

- **Do the group's goals and strategies exhibit a clear intention to build coproduction arrangements between community institutions and family institutions?** No matter what the area of concern, there are community institutions that could be working as productive partners with families and their networks. In the context of education, a local network of homeschooling families could be sharing online materials with the schools, enriching the curricula of those at home and those in formal classrooms. In the context of public safety, police departments and families could jointly ensure the presence of positive street activities that deter criminals. The key point here is to determine whether and how particular task forces are thinking in those terms and actively seeking alternative methods to support coproduction partnerships to realize their goals.

- **Does the planning group identify outcome measures that would clearly indicate improvements in the productive capacities of families?** Such groups can build into their projects efforts to track indicators of family productive capacity. In the economic development area, they could monitor local government data on business permits taken out by family enterprises. In the educational arena, they could collect from libraries aggregate data on the numbers of adults with enrolled children who borrow children's books. In the housing arena, data from the city planning department or board of realty could be tracked to monitor the stability of family ownership. Standard sets of indicators currently do not always measure how much families produce; they help measure the presence of assets available to families. Good planning projects will specify and track such indicators of performance; those bearing on family strengths can be integrated into the data sets already targeted for monitoring. Approaching the selection of indicators from the standpoint of family-generated community building can track new types of data that indicate the strength of family coproduction.

Practical Considerations

Community building is not a linear, reasoned process: the rational steps in solving problems take place in settings shaped by power struggles, conflicts of interest, deliberately obscured agendas, and unpredictable events. Thus, in addition to knowing how to inject the productive family into the rational process, one who advocates on behalf of family-generated community building must consider tactical variables that will shape problem definitions, goals, strategies, and outcomes. Of greatest relevance are leverage, timing, and training.

- **What are the pressure points where power must be leveraged to ensure serious consideration of the productive family and its institutions?** Are there ways in which the language in a problem statement is narrower than it ought to be? More particularly, whose interest is the narrow language protecting? And what leverage will it take to break the hold of that interest on the language? For example, imagine that a teachers' union has exerted such control over the problem statement of a group studying poor education outcomes that it mainly blames families for the problem. Who would be willing and able to at least partially displace the union from such a position of influence, thus enabling a broader, more realistic problem statement to be formulated? Perhaps the PTA, but many PTAs are devoted to advancing the concerns of teachers. Perhaps a mayor who is not beholden to teachers. This situation, which is not uncommon in local school politics, might require an organized effort on the part of families in a network operating autonomously from the school. The point is that power is used to shape problems, which in turn, delimit goals and strategies.

- **What relevant decision cycles must be taken into account to ensure that productive family institutions will be included in the strategies?** Community problem solving entails timing: government budget cycles, proposal due dates, legislative calendars, school district calendars, and many other institutional deadlines. Efforts to get support for productive family institutions and their networks must, like other strategies that arise from a community development project, be timed so that good-quality proposals are ready when government institutions and foundations are poised to receive them. If such proposals are somewhat outside the mainstream of what governmental bodies are used to considering, then it is even more important to approach their officials in advance with enough lead time to encourage an open-mindedness toward family enterprises and family-generated community building. Innovative programs must be worked through such channels with patience and tenacity. Knowing the decision cycles that officials must work with enables an advocate to approach them most effectively.

- **Does the process provide the necessary training for participants to ensure that they understand how building family-based strategies into their plans can help them realize their goals?** Family-generated community building is a unique approach, and it must not be assumed that participants from community institutions will automatically recognize the many productive roles that families can play in solving or preventing local problems. The family as a producer is different from the family as a consumer. Therefore, there must be intentional, well-designed efforts to provide training about recognizing family assets, knowing the kinds of productive institutions that families can create, and understanding how to build coproductive partnerships among families, schools, agencies, businesses, and local government. Making training available also signals to participants that family-generated community building is a framework valued by leaders of the project.

Evaluation

An evaluation must be designed to analyze both the process that shaped a community development effort and the outcomes that it produced. It will help ensure that staff members who will lead the implementation effort will be held accountable for achieving the community's objectives. Evaluations must include methods for gathering information and criteria for measuring success that are appropriate from the family-generated community building perspective.

- **Is the evaluation designed to measure credibly the impacts on the assets, institutions, and networks of families?** Referring to figure 3 (see chapter 3), one can see that family-generated community building enhances layers of assets and institutions around children. For example, does the evaluation measure the effects on families' financial assets, home ownership rates, farm foreclosure rates, family diets, garden output, business startups, and other indicators? Does the evaluation track impacts on family computer networks, business partnerships, cooperative purchasing networks, and housing or block associations?

• **Is the project designed so that evaluation results pertaining to family impacts will indeed be used to steer and, where necessary, change the project?** It is important that the evaluation's results be taken seriously by all relevant decision makers. Project leaders must be willing to act on the evaluation's results to alter their approaches, if necessary.

Collecting data on its own will not ensure that it will be fed back into the appropriate decision-making channels. The evaluation design must specify when outcome data will be generated, in what form, who will review them, and when they will make decisions based upon the data. This need for clear feedback channels pertains to all evaluation data, but is especially important for measures of a project's effect on families. Moreover, there must be methods built into the task force's or committee's work that will report evaluation findings to the larger community, as well as to advocates of productive family institutions. Such groups can provide leverage when necessary to ensure that the task force takes the family-related findings seriously and adjusts the project accordingly. (See chapter 8 for suggestions about the kinds of data that are germane to family-generated community building.)

The above questions deliver some guidance on how the community problem solving that takes place in localities throughout the year can be examined for its sensitivity to productive families and their institutions.

It is important to specify such questions because community development theory and practice have never really adapted rigorously to the transformation of the family from a producing to a consuming institution. Ironically, as has been argued above, strong and healthy communities around children cannot really emerge unless families can function as producers, as well as consumers.

If a community is not organized to make its planning processes attentive to the productive family, then it is leaving one of its most important institutions severely underused. Unfortunately, this is currently the case in most localities. The formal institutions and their leaders tend to define *themselves* as "the community" when they gather. They involve parents as consumers only. They might survey parents as consumers for their preferences about the goods and services that the institutions provide them. But, in shortsighted fashion, they have tended to ignore the family as a coproducer of education, business development, safety, physical health, mental health, environmental cleanliness, and many other good things that they seek through community development.

A good audit of current community development efforts using the above questions can make those efforts more likely to achieve their process goals as well as their outcomes. Community development is not only about producing programmatic outcomes, but it is also meant to create social stability and healthy bonds among citizens as a direct by-product of the interactions that it fosters. Family-generated community building adds important criteria to weigh when assessing how community problem-solving efforts are working. The criteria lead one to ask about how the productive capacities of families are strengthened as a by-product as well.

Engaging families as producers rather than consumers only is of paramount importance if community problem-solving on a whole range of issues is to succeed. Families as producers add the following to the process:

- Arguments and information about what problem is to be addressed;
- Ideas for solutions;
- Enterprises and institutions that can implement solutions, either on their own or as coproducers with nonfamilial institutions;
- Ideas about how they can help nonfamilial institutions work more effectively;
- Support services and settings for meetings;
- Networks through which information can flow and participation of others can be encouraged; and
- Ideas, information, and settings for observation and meetings to aid in the evaluation process.

When they are so engaged, the community as a whole is fully together.

CHAPTER 8

Putting Family-Generated
Community Building into Practice

What would a community look like if it were teeming with the kinds of productive families that it needed? If a community embarked on a planning and development process aimed at building the productive capacities of families, what measurable indicators would it pursue? Who would be responsible for achieving these indicators? How would they do it?

What Would Such a Place Look Like?

A community blessed with a rich, diverse array of productive families would see them active in business activities, recreation, education, food production, safety, and other arenas important to their quality of life.

Some businesses would be operated from homes. For example, there would be repair shops in garages attached to homes or close enough that the distance between them would foster easy connections. Such shops would fix bikes, cars, appliances, furniture, homes, garages, fences, and other things. Within the domain of home repair there would be plumbers, carpenters, dry wall experts, painters, flooring specialists, and electricians.

In the food arena, there would be family enterprises functioning as bakeries, breakfast cafes, small or medium-sized grocers, taverns, and restaurants. Some families would be growing food for themselves, for sharing with others, or for sale to local restaurants and grocers. Or they might sell their produce through a local farmers' market.

The growing might take place in raised beds in backyards, on lots shared by different households, or in larger community gardens worked by many families and individuals. Enough homes would be equipped to store tools, supplies, and the produce itself. Rain barrels and composting devices would be evident on many properties. Some family habitats and shared garden spaces would also have apiaries that produced honey and facilitated pollination of fruit and vegetable plants by the bees dwelling in them.

Also evident in the community would be families active in recreation as coaches, association leaders, umpires, fundraisers, field caretakers, scorekeepers, vendors, and of course, participants. Fathers might be coaching baseball or soccer teams. Mothers might be coaching basketball. Older siblings and parents might jointly coach the teams of younger players.

Of course, recreation includes more than just competitive sports. There might be playgroups for young children staffed in part by mothers, aunts, or siblings. Dance workshops might be led similarly. Such activities could take place in municipal parks, schools, fields owned by churches, or in spaces owned by nonprofit organizations.

What might the community look like if it were also teeming with families playing productive roles in education? Some children would be homeschooled, perhaps through the elementary years or maybe through high school. Other children might be schooled in part at home and in part at the formal schools, public and otherwise. Even if the majority of children were attending a formal school, mothers and fathers would be evident in the schools as guest teachers, monitors, and members of committees with meaningful roles in the school.

When a community is educating its children well, as much of the teaching and learning takes place outside of the schools as inside them. Homes would be functioning as teaching and learning centers. Some teaching would be explicitly educational as when parents read to their children, teaching them vocabulary and grammar in the process. Much teaching would be informal, taking place as a by-product of conversations about goings on in the neighborhood, television shows, movies, music, and politics.

Many children and adults would be learning and practicing their crafts as musicians or artists in their homes. Some piano teachers would base their studios or businesses at home. Students learning instruments would practice mostly in their homes, encouraged by their parents. Even when lessons themselves took place outside the homes, most of the learning and skill building would result from practice in them.

Religious education, even when delivered formally in church or school, would be internalized through conversations and prayer in the homes. This would be the case no matter what the faith might be. Prayer might include words before a meal or meditation in one's room. It might involve contemplation of a statue, painting, or other symbol. Prayer would be reinforced through literature and conversations about the development of faith, the differences among faiths, and the relevance of faith to daily interactions with friends, teachers, or neighbors.

In a community in which families are present due to their business, gardening, social, recreational, or educational activities, they are also more consistently present to prevent, deter, or report criminal activity. Children would walk home from school through neighborhoods and down commercial streets where they would be known, observed, and therefore safer. The light cast by many eyes on the streets from homes, gardens, shops, and schools would be a natural deterrent to criminals. It would also serve as a force without which police could not be effective, no matter how many cameras might be installed in public areas.[69]

It would be possible to go on and on with more examples of what a community looks like when it is full of many kinds of productive families. For example, we could enumerate the many ways that families provide health care, both in the preventive sense and in the delivery context. After surgery, most healing takes place at home. After the doctor prescribes medication for a virus or infection, most of the administration of the medicine, the rest, the monitoring, and other forms of care are delivered at home in family relationships. Despite the imposing budgets and massive technologies involved in hospitals and clinics, their professionals are not in the end the most numerous health care providers: families are.

Indicators of Family-Generated Community Building

Indicators are quantitative statements about what would constitute the success of a community-building endeavor. Community building is an intentional process. It might be initiated by grass roots organizers, by municipal planners, or by new policy initiatives. But, however it starts, it must engage all layers—inside and outside, formal and informal—together. Thus, because it involves different institutions and actors with somewhat different interests and perspectives, it is necessary to establish agreement on the desired community outcomes.

Outcomes for a process meant to strengthen productive families, even as it also strives to improve education or economic conditions, must therefore identify the indicators for the desired results at the family level. Family-generated community building must therefore begin with indicators of productive family life.

---

69 In fact, neighborhood beat officers are trained to cultivate ties with people who are present in their areas routinely. They back one another up. They share information. The residents and shopkeepers make the officers feel welcome; the officers build trust with the families, and the spaces in which crimes might occur become scarce as a result.

While not exhaustive, the following list enumerates examples of such indicators:

- **The number of enterprises owned and operated by families.** These could be subdivided into:
  - Home-based enterprises
    - Enterprises in the homes
    - Enterprises in garages or spaces on the same property as homes
  - Home-linked enterprises
- **The number of enterprises owned and operated by families in various business areas.**[70] Some examples could include:
  - Restaurants and cafes
  - Repair services (which can be further broken down into types of repair provided)
  - Studios
  - Grocers
  - Food production
  - Health care
  - Child care
  - Administrative support services
- **The number of enterprises employing multiple family members**, including those working:
  - Full time
  - Part time
- **The number of non-family members employed by family enterprises**, including those working:
  - Full time
  - Part time
- **Average annual sales generated by different types of family enterprises**, broken down into categories like those enumerated above.
- **The number of family enterprises in operation** for:
  - One year or less
  - Between one and three years
  - Three years or longer

---

70   Extensive, well organized descriptions of many types of home-based enterprises can be found in the works cited previously: Paul and Sarah Edwards, op. cit., 2002; Paul and Sarah Edwards, op. cit., 2004; Christine Durst and Michael Haaren, op. cit., 2005.

- **The number of family-operated fruit and vegetable gardens.** More particular data items would describe the following characteristics:
  - Home-based gardens
  - Home-linked gardens
  - Shared garden spaces
  - Square footage of productive space
  - Pounds of produce processed annually
    - Types of fruits
    - Types of vegetables
  - Square footage in production for family's own use
  - Square footage in production for sale
  - Square footage in production for exchange or sharing
  - Numbers of apiaries and hives
- **The number of homeschooling families**
  - Number of children being homeschooled
  - Number of children by grade level
- **The number of co-schooling families (partly homeschooled and partly taught in formal schools)**
  - Number of children
  - Number of children by grade level
    - In math
    - In science
    - In social studies
    - In humanities
    - In language
- **The number of parents in teaching and service roles in schools,** including those serving:
  - In classrooms
  - Outside of classrooms
  - In elementary schools
  - In middle schools
  - In high schools
  - During school hours
  - After school hours
- **The number of homes in which musical instruction takes place**
- **Percentage of children with parents home after school**
  - Before 6:00 p.m.

- After 6:00 p.m.
- **Percentage of families with working, up-to-date computers at home**
- **Percentage of families with Internet connectivity at home**

Of course, the existence of enterprises, the presence of gardens, the evidence of schooling, and the availability of computers in homes does not, on its own, prove that families are functioning effectively and efficiently with any of these resources. Such indicators are not intended to tell the full story of how much families are contributing to the generation of community. They do, however, provide tangible bases for setting goals and determining strategies that could not only increase their numbers but also bolster their functioning.

Who Is Responsible and How?

Ensuring that a community is enriched by many types of productive family enterprises and habitats takes a commitment on the part of various informal and formal institutions. These institutions must do their parts individually as well as collectively through planning. They are made up of the families themselves (especially parents), local anchor institutions, coproduction networks, local government, and state government.

The process through which these entities work together must be place-based, that is, focused on concentrated development within a geographically coherent neighborhood, village, or district whose identity is meaningful to the locality. It must be ongoing and guided by shared goals and outcomes that are agreed upon in advance. It can be initiated by families themselves acting as leaders, by institutions with legitimacy in the area, by the local government, or at times, more loosely by the state or federal government. But, no matter who initiates the process, the *buy-in* for it must be evident at all levels.

Families

In every community, there are certain families who are known for having operated successful enterprises or for having created service projects that give them legitimacy as leaders. They might run hardware stores, cafes, auto repair shops, or home-based child care centers successfully. Through the networks they form in operating these concerns, they make many friends; they get to know the needs and interests of people; and they gain respect through their examples of competence. They can already speak to the benefits that their families derive from having managed their enterprises.

Such family-enterprise builders—fathers, mothers, grandmothers, or grandfathers—often become leaders in their communities due to the stature that having their businesses provides. They can testify at government hearings, they weigh in on zoning or traffic plans that will impact their areas of service or markets, and they often serve on local commissions or boards. They are in a good position to say to their communities, "We, as a village (or neighborhood), need to empower more families to start successful enterprises." Often when the impetus for a planning process comes from people like this, others listen.

Thus, families themselves can instigate the community development process needed to spawn new family enterprises. The credibility they bring to the table by virtue of having done it themselves gets others to listen. The legitimacy they bring to a forum because of the networks they have established raises the comfort level among members of boards or commissions that these community leaders speak for important interests in the community.

Families can spur the process to begin, and they can participate as leaders. However, they can also contribute by initiating their own enterprises and keeping them connected to the community.

In fact, there is no substitute for the proactive efforts of families. They have to decide for themselves the kinds of enterprises or projects they want to create. They must create the business plans—study market conditions, choose the kinds of products or services they will offer, study their competition, acquire space, build space, arrange financing, set up books, delineate roles for management and production, open bank accounts, and many other things. They must reach out to potential customers, partners, or clients. They have to approach local governments for the proper permits. They might have to go to the state government to incorporate. If they are creating service projects, they will seek grants or donations. In all this activity, families are not only organizing themselves, they are also extending their energies into the community. In their own modest ways, one by one, they are helping to build it.

Community Anchor Institutions

In order that communities can ensure that they receive the goods and services they need from families, they must weave into their own institutional fabrics, their plans, and their policies, ways to draw on core local assets to help sustain productive households. They can do so by making the critical anchor institutions supportive of productive families and productive family habitats.

Community anchor institutions are entities that, because of statutory commitments, deep cultural ties to a place, or stable financial assets, do not move out even when the population changes or changes in commercial markets lead residents or businesses to move. These institutions are already rooted more deeply than most to the places themselves. For example, they include schools, municipal service centers, community colleges, some universities, and in some cases where the ties to property and community culture are durable, nonprofit community centers. In some places, especially in Catholic neighborhoods where the parish style of organization is used, the churches and their schools might also serve as community anchor institutions. In certain cases, hospitals or health care campuses might also serve as community anchor institutions.

These entities are *anchor* institutions because of their political, cultural, or fiscal ties to the places where they operate. They are important to the communities because they help them weather change and provide them a base of financial, physical, and cultural assets embedded in place. They are important to—and dependent on—families because of the coproductive capacities that families must lend to help them achieve their goals.

Such anchor institutions can further family-generated community building by hosting families, community leaders, planners, funders, and others with a stake in the place in the planning and development forums. In addition, they can put resources on the table that could further the programmatic actions that might be selected by such planning groups. They might be able to make financial contributions to projects.

More particularly, they can offer a variety of partnership opportunities, contracting opportunities, technical assistance, and financial support to productive family enterprises. For example, a hospital might contract laundry, cleaning, or grounds keeping services from family enterprises in the community. A school might contract after-school care with family enterprises (to take place in the school or in the homes). Similar to the hospitals, schools might contract laundry, cleaning, and grounds keeping with family enterprises in the area.

More schools could work with families as coeducators, or in what has been referred to here as co-schooling. In co-schooling, parents with the proper educational backgrounds teach a course or two to their children at home and the schools cover the other coursework in the formal classrooms. There are many parents who are well educated enough to teach elementary social studies, language, math, sciences, and other subjects. Online resources for homeschooling are abundant. Internet connections can enable easy communications between the home "classroom" and the school classroom.

A community development process hosted in a school could delve into such possibilities for the coproduction of education. Charter schools are already intended to foster broader partnerships between parents and teachers. Why not enable communities to set goals for getting families more invested in education by supporting a certain percentage of them in such co-schooling partnerships?

The home might be a particularly suitable classroom for children with disabilities. The home might be more physically accessible to them. It might offer fewer distractions for children with learning disabilities that make it hard to focus on learning tasks.

Whereas schools could serve as anchors for certain kinds of productive family activities, other institutions could be helpful in other domains. A community bank, credit union, or development corporation could provide technical assistance and financing for family enterprises. A community bank could offer workshops for family enterprises on how to acquire financing. A community college could team with the bank to provide training on the development of sound business plans.

The college or perhaps a community development corporation could set up incubator space for new family enterprises. An incubator would provide not only space, but *appropriately designed* spaces, electrical and Internet connections, perhaps the needed kitchen facilities, and other infrastructure that could help a fledgling business navigate its start-up phase of operations.

All of the above programs are already operated by some such institutions. But, they are usually not organized to work together. A community development process aiming at family-generated community building would integrate such efforts, enlisting the resources of local anchor institutions, and concentrating them in the desired places.

As described above, some coproduction and support activities involving productive families and anchor institutions would entail the organization of *coproduction networks*. In the example of the banks and community colleges working with family enterprises, we see the need for such networks in the economic development arena. Families receiving the training could be connected with one another and the institutions through a network, furthering their ability to provide mutual assistance. Similarly, with respect to the coproduction of education, family enterprises serving the schools, co-schooling parents, and the professional teachers could form networks that make educational resources available, keep schedules up-to-date, solve other problems, and generally keep information accessible to all.

By envisioning such networks, it is possible to see how individual family production in the economic, educational, or other areas also stirs community building. The relationships forged through the networks can foster a sense of common interest and purpose. The interactions among families and anchor institutions would yield social capital and further the organization of assets that undergird the community's as well as the individual family's viability. The learning fostered through technical assistance and educational activities builds up the community's capacity to generate more of its own goods and services. In this process, families would generate community building as well as good things for themselves.

Government

The closer the level of government is to the community, the more directly it can enter into the process as a participant or facilitator. All layers of government—local, state, and federal—can be helpful, but in different ways:

The **city or town government** is in the best position to: initiate the planning process for family-generated community building; strategically choose how to inject resources into a process initiated by other local institutions; or adapt local codes to make the formation of productive family enterprises and habitats easy to do. It is in the best position because the local municipality is itself one of the community's productive institutions. Its elected officials and the party organizations that back them are part of the local community. Even when the community of focus represents only some of the territory in the municipality (a smaller neighborhood in the village, for example), the local government might have ward-based representation or geographic service districts (police, fire, and others) that align closely with the community's boundaries. In fact, it is in the mutual interests of the community and the local government to foster family-generated community building, because so much of the family production that results—economic development, safety, property upkeep, maintenance of property values (and therefore the local tax base)—is necessary for the local government's viability.

A city or town can initiate family-generated community building by making it central to either its comprehensive planning process or to the development of sub-area plans. Family enterprises, habitats, and coproduction networks can be central to any of the policy domains that would be included in such municipal plans. For example, in the housing section of a plan, data collection, hearings, and other means of gathering data can inquire into the current uses of housing by families for business or food production. Planners can study how current housing or land available for housing is designed or amenable for enterprises. Some housing might be developed as live/work units. New developments might be designed so that there are shared spaces for family enterprises or gardens.

Similarly, with respect to the economic development section of a plan, staff or committees involved in devising strategies might consider how tax credits, small loans, or grants might be made to support the location of family vegetable or family bakery kiosks in larger supermarkets or malls. Due to location incentives that they often provide, local governments often hold some leverage with major supermarkets and other businesses over possible uses of their space.

Government can offer similar incentives in planning mixed-use housing and commercial spaces. Technical assistance also might be made available. These incentives ensure that a certain percentage of new spaces—housing and commercial—are taken up by families who live in, and operate enterprises in, such spaces.[71]

In such planning at the comprehensive or area level, municipalities play the lead roles. Planning departments' own staff often generate the initial plans that become the focus of debate and critique by citizens and commissions. The municipalities might also contract out planning and design work to private firms. But even when the technical work involved in planning is executed by private firms, the contract terms set by the municipalities can specify that assessments, goals, and ultimately, the resulting planning strategies include very deliberate efforts to foster productive family enterprises and habitats.

When the development process is led by a community organization or anchor institution, rather than by the city, the municipality still has much to contribute to the build-up of family enterprises and other productive roles for families. Consider a situation in which a community, led by a coalition of human service organizations and churches, is aiming to lower the risks that youths face from violence and substance abuse. Although the city might not be playing the convening role, it might still make available the following resources in order to buttress the productive roles that families can play in lowering the risks facing young people. The city could:

- Through the police department, foster a home-based network of safe houses and neighborhood-watch liaisons so that more families kept their eyes on the streets and were in close contact with neighborhood beat officers, and so that children knew where they could go if they felt threatened.
- Concentrate efforts to train and capitalize family enterprises and productive habitats in certain areas where more of a constant family presence was needed.
- Tear down abandoned, rundown buildings and assist families to reuse the properties for food production, thereby taking away spaces friendly to dangerous purposes such as drug-dealing and

---

71 See Tom Dolan's Live/Work Institute at www.live-work.com/lwi/ for examples of projects that combine these goals.

replacing them with spaces controlled by families for positive uses.

- Offer tax credits to families who put solar-powered lighting on their homes, garages, parking slabs, and other structures, lowering their exposure to crime or drug activity.

The above examples represent positive actions that municipalities can take even when the community-building process is led by an organization other than itself. Consider how valuable they would be to an effort led by a church or community center that might be triggered by substance abuse or violence involving youth. Ensuring that more families are home and watching their neighborhoods, eliminating dangerous buildings, and increasing home lighting would also reduce the risk factors that expose youth to these maladies.

A third cluster of actions that municipalities can take to foster family-generated community building is found in the regulations and codes that govern the use of land, the functions of buildings, and the uses of other public and private spaces. Many municipalities are finding the need to update their zoning codes to accommodate the rapid increase in home-based work. Many homes are becoming mixed-use spaces—business and residential—even when the homes themselves are still zoned strictly for residential purposes. New mixes of uses and restrictions can allow home offices or home kitchens that are partly used for serving customers. Building codes for live/work units that might provide residential space on an upper floor and business space—a studio or salon—on the first floor would need to specify how the building should be wired electrically or provided the ventilation that would be appropriate for the business and living spaces.

Allowing for the use of land zoned for single-family homes for agricultural activities—growing, watering, moving produce from the small farm to the market—requires zoning attentive to foot traffic, the tilling of land, access for trucks, storage, composting, and other activities, even as the overall residential character of the area would be maintained.

As the unit of government closest to the communities where the productive capacities of families must flourish, the city, town, township, or even county is most responsible for this form of community building. These kinds of municipalities are also best positioned to benefit from increased family production.

States and the federal government can also offer many resources to further family-generated community building. Because the benefits of concentrating different types of federal and state programs in targeted places are attractive, many comprehensive community initiatives have been attempted during the past several decades. These efforts are fraught with difficulties, given the fragmentation among different programs, the obstacles posed by multiple jurisdictions, and often the perceived lack of legitimacy of federal and state officials who come to localities with aims to improve them from the outside.

Nevertheless, even when administering policies from the state or federal level, it is better to concentrate multiple component projects (those that pursue interrelated improvements in schools, economic development, housing, environmental remediation, and others) in places instead of scattering specialized grants in isolated initiatives across many areas of a state or region. That is because concentrating them in particular neighborhoods, villages, or regions enables local leaders and citizens to ensure that they can be linked and mutually reinforcing. The place and its institutions, including those in governance and service delivery, serve as a kind of integrative matrix for linking diverse projects. And where the focus is to be on place-based, concentrated initiatives, the build-up of productive family capacities, roles, habitats, and institutions must be central to the effort.

Localities with good plans for geographic communities and their productive family enterprises will be able to work better with state and federal initiatives that are comprehensive and targeted. For example, when a state or federal initiative offers a package of housing, economic development, and environmental remediation grants for coordinated efforts at community revitalization, the communities that have already developed their own plans will be ahead of the game and better able to use these resources effectively. They will be able to apply them to family-generated community building if they already have the kinds of local strategies in place described above.

On the other hand, a comprehensive state or federal initiative can be a clumsy and inefficient resource when introduced to a community where good plans are not already in place. First, the state or federal programs being offered are themselves complicated, limited by restrictions spelled out in statutes, and difficult to integrate with one another. Second, when there is a local planning vacuum, any projects, plans, and development capacities locally needed to make the best use of these resources from above will not be available quickly enough. Third, without a concerted local effort to ready a community to foster productive family enterprises and habitats, there will be little context in which to use grants, loans, and credits from above to support them. Family-generated community building must begin locally. No matter how well intentioned, state and federal programs cannot foster family-generated community building without a good base of local planning.[72]

Summary

To ensure that communities get the most benefit from the productive capacities of families, they must intentionally plan to support them. This planning must begin with the collection of data about the current productive assets, enterprises, habitats, and networks of families. It must be deliberate, following through with the definition of clear outcomes, well designed projects, and continuous assessments of how effectively those projects are operating. Each level of a community's decision-making needs to be engaged, including families themselves, community anchor institutions, local governments, and state and federal governments. Governments do not have to lead the community-building process. In fact, it is best if the state and federal government try not to. Their resources can best be put to use when the elements of local community building are already in place: positive family involvement, leadership from local institutions, support or even periodic leadership from municipalities, and good plans already in place.

---

72   For a description and analysis of a comprehensive, place-based initiative that the author directed, see Richard S. Kordesh, "Mistakes in Place: The Premature Termination of Illinois Workforce Advantage," in Robert Giloth and Colin Austin, *Mistakes to Success: Learning and Adapting When Things Go Wrong* (New York: iUniverse), 2010, 185–203. See also Maureen Hellwig, *Illinois Workforce Advantage: An Experiment in Place-Based Government/Community Partnerships* (Chicago, IL: Policy Research Action Group, Loyola University), 2002.

CHAPTER 9
Obstacles and Openings

This analysis seeks to improve community development theory and practice, especially as they bear on strengthening the community around children. It argues that a variety of factors over many years has pushed parents out of the thick, productive roles that their children need them to play. Several different layers of action must take place simultaneously at the governmental, community, organizational, and personal levels to effect these needed changes in the relationship between families and community building. The community development approach that represents these steps taken together we have referred to as *family-generated community building.*

Family-generated community building will strengthen parents' relationships with one another and with their children. It will encourage and protect the thick, multidimensional roles that can result. It will press for community institutions and policy institutions to help families acquire decent housing that would then foster productive family activities.

It would work with schools to build coproductive relationships with parents, including training for parents who needed to enhance their own literacy skills. Family-generated community building would assist families in working with the land on their properties and in their neighborhoods, enabling them to improve their diets, offset their expenses, and generally gain more control of their lives through family and community gardening.

The community of place is critically important for children. However, a focus on place is not enough: within the places that are targeted for community development, productive roles for parents and productive family institutions must be supported.

As figure 5 illustrates, family-generated community building integrates the generic steps in place-based community development with new strategies devoted to building productive family institutions and roles. Building community around children necessitates not just organizing diverse formal resources within places, but also making sure that, in those places, families are enabled to form their own enterprises.

Policies that take a value-added rather than wholly prescriptive approach to community development are necessary. Value-added approaches begin with the integrity of local plans and aspirations and then find the means (within the law) through grants, tax credits, regulatory actions, and other actions to strengthen the capacities of communities to realize their goals. On the other hand, prescriptive approaches are designed wholly in advance at the federal or state level and force upon the localities goals, objectives, program designs, and evaluation criteria that may or not may not match up with community assets and liabilities.

Among the institution-building efforts to which policies must add value are family businesses, cooperatives, networks of family enterprises, family gardens, family farms, and new coproductive partnerships between families and schools. An intensive focus on place, in other words, is necessary, but not sufficient, to build good communities around children. In those places, productive family institutions must emerge.

Why Is Family-Generated Community Building *Not* Happening?

A number of obstacles exist that make it difficult to conduct family-generated community building. Some arise from contemporary culture, others from an absence of skills, and others from entrenched and powerful interests. Still other impediments reside in narrow or rigid ways of thinking. Let us consider the last of these first.

1) The family debate in the United States is stuck in outmoded, predictable, ideological boxes. The debate over whether the family is in decline or merely changing tends to obscure any concern over the fate of the *productive* family. And the productive family is the key to empowering, and therefore protecting, the family. Liberals react defensively when confronted with criticism of government social programs. This is especially true when such programs are blamed by conservatives for causing the family's decline, as for example, when women could not receive public assistance if a man lived with her and her children. This defensiveness explains in part the reticence of too many liberals to promote the two-parent family or criticize the single-parent (usually mother) family. For their part, conservatives generally attack vociferously the welfare state and its impacts on the family, but turn a blind eye toward the terrible destruction that business corporations have leveled on families, such as the withdrawal of the automobile industry from Detroit or the industrialization of farming.

Thus, it becomes very difficult to penetrate the public policy agenda with anything other than a "knee-jerk" liberal or "half-blind" conservative perspective on policy design. Yet, real families are out there in cities, towns, and rural communities struggling to form new businesses and maintain their farms. Despite the high failure rate, many men and women continue to marry and remarry. Many surveys show that they want more time for their family roles and more control of their lives. People want family. People want strong families.

Yet liberals still call for the endless expansion of agencies and programs that have helped to dilute the family's productive capacities. Conservatives still call for shifting more power to business corporations. Both ignore the underlying problem; both have bolstered each other in displacing the family from its productive roles, thinning motherhood and fatherhood, and generally diverting parents from relationships with their children.

2) Narrow conceptions of productivity and work prevent many fathers from rebuilding satisfying, productive roles. Traditional prejudices about what constitutes manly work keep many marginally employable men from making contributions to their families' well-being. The conception of the home needs to evolve from the modern view as a place only for residential consumption and childrearing to a post-modern view as a place of work and productivity, broadly defined, that sustains its habitants. Although this is probably changing slowly, mothers more than fathers still seek to balance work and family life by working from home.

One very fruitful area in which to make more productive use of the home is family agriculture—rural and urban. Those vast numbers of men in low-income neighborhoods whose correctional backgrounds and lack of formal education keep them from good jobs could be taking the lead in creating new, urban agricultural enterprises. When networked with one another, such urban farmers could pool their energies and harvests and even market their vegetables, herbs, and fruits to local restaurants and groceries. Working the land needs to be recognized as dignified work, worthy of a strong man dedicated to a productive partnership with his employed spouse.

Fathers who work from home control their time more than those who work in more distant offices. They find it easier to make room to coach youth sports teams, pick up their young ones from school, and be there when the school calls about an emergency. They can keep their eyes on the streets and prevent crime.

Before they were lured into factories and corporate offices—in other words, for most of recorded history up to little over a hundred years ago—fathers were at home to work, and their work at home thickened their roles as fathers. Today's fathers can create new ways to work and to be home as they embrace mutually dignified partnerships with the mothers of their children.

3) Powerful, entrenched interests depend on thin parenthood and its counterpart, the consumer family. Entire retail sectors and industries, food and agriculture among them, owe their existence to the family in its thin, reactive state. Despite the efforts to increase "parent involvement," school administrators and professional teachers still depend on controlling the substance and methods of education. In fact, the new accountability mechanisms that evaluate schools through standardized tests only drive teachers into less flexible modes of teaching. The parent-choice movement in education annoys teachers, but ironically further institutionalizes the parent as consumer in education.

4) Hyperindividualism of the kind feared by Tocqueville flourishes today in modern forms and rationalizes weak family and marital commitments. The dreaded *egoism* that the great analyst of American culture worried over thrives within and among us. It is trumpeted and celebrated in commercial advertising. Entire industries thrive on its impulses. Even the housing industry has grown dependent on it: more people choose to live alone than at any point in our history. This drives up housing demand, housing scarcity, housing prices, and, lamentably for families, feeds the crisis of affordability.

Fueled by consumerism, egoistic energies flourish in electoral politics as never before. The decline in party loyalties is not just a sign that voters and candidates are more discerning and thoughtful in their views. Rather, it is a sign that loyalty itself—to place, to philosophy, to group—is a diminishing factor in politics.

Religion, which Tocqueville and the framers of the Constitution assumed would help counterbalance egoism, has instead been reshaped by it. Consider the competition among churches to entertain rather than check the tendency toward ego centeredness among their members.

5) Illiteracy among the poor is perpetuated by family breakdown, and then makes productive family life more difficult to sustain. No society has ever been able to transmit linguistic abilities from one generation to the next without intact families. Parents are still the most important teachers of language. When they are too disengaged from their children to talk with them, read to them, and explain the immediate world to them, the transmission of literacy is severed.

When parents are themselves unable to read and write well enough to teach their children, the cycle of education failure and poverty continues beyond them into the lives of their offspring. The family-as-teacher must be bolstered, and it is right for schools and family-resource centers to emphasize family literacy. It is right to bridge education into financial literacy, and it would be even more effective as an antipoverty measure to teach business and agricultural literacy. Then families could broaden their productive capacities through their own institutions.

6) Populist political philosophy, which is needed to galvanize political forces around productive family institutions, is in a marginalized, discredited state of affairs. Populism today tends to mean either a left-wing cultural radicalism that views marriage and family as marginally important institutions, or a right-wing radicalism that fosters resentment toward recent immigrant groups. In contrast, populism should represent a commitment to ensuring that small institutions play productive roles in the economy, in politics, and generally in society. Moreover, populist philosophy should uplift the critically important roles that productive family institutions play in stabilizing communities, keeping the economy sound, and helping to maintain a vital political democracy.

Populism's roots go deep in American political history, and those roots need to be unearthed in order to recognize the dignified place that productive family institutions have long been accorded in our national identity.

Jeffersonian politics in the late eighteenth and early nineteenth centuries assumed the presence of family institutions. The agrarian populists of the late nineteenth century fought the last great, national political battle on behalf of family farmers. After the 1896 election, the tide of political change moved against them, but populism never died. It never will, because the interests of mothers, fathers, and small productive institutions are intertwined.

Unfortunately, interests in education, business, and social welfare that have been fed by the turnaround of the family from producer to consumer dominate political organizing in the mainstream. Restoring the productive family's central place in populist thinking will move populism back to a more dignified role in politics. It would also generate policies that would nurture, protect, and underwrite productive family roles and institutions (for more on populism and contending political viewpoints, see chapter 10).

7) Community development theory as it is today tends to obscure the family's unique role in places; it treats family as just another group, or does not explicitly recognize it at all. To advocate on behalf of marginalized people in low-income communities is essential, but should not obscure the fact that part of the process of helping them get off the margins will be through the rebuilding of productive family institutions. Community development theory that is consumer oriented has grown naturally out of work in neighborhoods where family life is tenuous, where single parenthood has become a norm, where fathers are more likely to be unemployed, and many are disengaged from their children.

As they should, community organizers seek to start with people where they are and, thus, are reticent to impose upon them rhetoric about the family that would seem to fit better in a stable, middle-class neighborhood. However, rhetoric about the family does not have to promote consumerist values; it can promote an empowerment perspective reflective of populist values. Building family institutions must be recognized as an essential element of empowerment.

There are community development efforts that promote microenterprises, home-based child care, community gardening, and other productive local endeavors. Yet even these in many cases take the makeup of the household—usually a single-parent mother—as a given, without taking the next step of engaging fathers in the same enterprises or at least teaching young men who have yet to bring children into the world that such family institutions are also their responsibility to create in partnerships with young women.

Community development practitioners and theoreticians must put themselves on the line in defense of the productive family—mother, father, children, and other members who could be present. There will be no stable communities around children if the men who give them life are not joined with their mothers in productive, empowering institutions.

As figure 5 depicts, there can be a rich, mutual dependency between family-generated community building and the steps followed by place-based community development. The latter is usually led by elite, formal institutions such as cities, regional planning bodies, collaborative planning bodies formed at the behest of foundations, or formal organizations empowered by federal grants. When they are being effective, they are integrating plans and policies around the shared goals established for improving the economies, social characteristics, environmental conditions, or educational outcomes in locally meaningful geographic areas.

Yet, all of these depend for their achievement on a sustainable effort from families as coproducers. The process of family-generated community building articulated in chapter 4 must take place in a way that is aligned with, and transforms in structure and purpose, the formal collaboratives. Family institutions must be strengthened and engaged; they must be interlinked in the formation of networks; their enterprises must be bolstered internally; and their productive assets must be built up. Then, they will be able to contribute to place-based development as coplanners and coproducers with the formal systems.

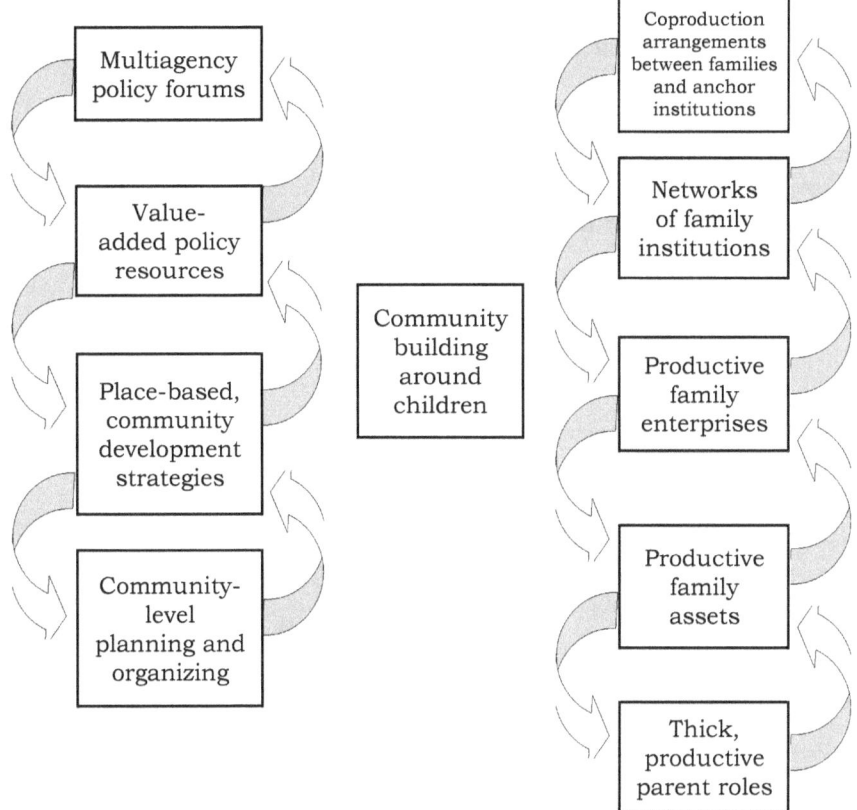

Figure 5: A Model of Family-Generated Community Building
as Complementary to the Place-Based Approach

Where Are the Best Opportunities for Furthering Family-Generated Community Building?

A number of initiatives and movements are underway whose principles or strategies are compatible with the tenets of family-generated community building. Family-generated community building could in fact further these efforts were it to be embraced by them.

1) In addition to the large numbers already in existence, there are vast numbers of housing developments and *common-interest communities* being built in the United States. Private community associations will govern most of them. Thus, they enjoy the leeway to write their charters with the explicit intention to engage families as decision makers, to encourage the integration of work into the home and habitat, and to form networks of families around such tasks as farming and educating children.

These associations have been criticized—justifiably—for their isolated, exclusionary powers and for their tendency to emphasize tedious and trivial matters of internal governance.[73] Yet private-housing communities are a growing part of the residential landscape, and there is no sign of their abatement.

The principles of family-generated community building could make them better places for children, more democratic, and better integrated with their surrounding places. For instance:

- Community associations could build productive roles for family institutions into their plans for landscaping, maintenance, recreational programming, and other community activities. As it is, middle-class associations tend to contract out most services; residents play few productive roles in the design and maintenance of their common spaces.
- Municipal governments and state governments could require that new private communities engage in place-based community development planning with surrounding neighborhoods and municipalities, preventing them from becoming isolated worlds unto themselves. Those plans should include strategies for fostering productive family enterprises and productive family roles in planning, education, and other matters that are addressed as items of mutual interest.
- Community associations could foster local democracy by creating community networks among their residents, including the families. This would strengthen the sense of mutual interest and attachment to their places. Families—as families—could be given a greater stake in planning by being linked into cross-household conversations about community issues.

In short, as community associations are pressed to become more democratic, more integrated with their surrounding areas, and less exclusionary, the roles of parents and children can change through physical and organizational design as well. Productive roles for families and their institutions must be built into their planning, upkeep, and decision making.

---

73   Evan McKenzie, *Privatopias: Homeowner Associations and the Rise of Residential Private Government* (New Haven, CT: Yale University Press), 1994.

2) *New urbanist* designs for communities can make more explicit recognition of the roles that productive family institutions can play in building a sense of place and in fostering mixed-use spaces. The new urbanism is a movement in architecture and planning that draws on many of the design elements inherent in the older, urban neighborhoods of Boston, New York, Chicago, Baltimore, and San Francisco.[74] Those elements include walkability; functional integration of commercial, residential, and recreational spaces; ease of access to public transit; use of common spaces such as squares and markets to facilitate human interaction; and the use of alleys, front porches, and other features. In fact, new urbanism grew in part out of a negative reaction to isolated, single-use residential communities that have proliferated in expanding suburban areas.

Curiously, given its celebration of the older neighborhoods, new urbanism has not brought forward the central roles they created for productive family enterprises. As noted in a previous chapter, the family shop and its attached residence was a common feature intentionally built into places such as Boston's North End and Chicago's Lawndale neighborhoods. That those neighborhoods worked in establishing a sense of place was due in part to the fact that they helped ground the work lives, the social lives, and the spiritual lives of families in those areas.

Why not make the establishment of functionally integrated family spaces one of the favored design elements in the new urbanist agenda? A visit to the old neighborhoods from which new urbanism draws its thinking and the new communities where its principles are being applied will show that families are indeed still striving to integrate their work lives and social lives through the creative use of those very spaces. This is as true in Chicago's Little Village (formerly known as South Lawndale), where family enterprises exist everywhere, as it is in suburban Oak Park, where home businesses and home offices are growing daily in number.

In addition to the new directions that are shaping planning, other opportunities for furthering family-generated community building exist in today's social movements. These include the efforts of "family support" advocates, promoters of marriage, and resurgent advocacy on behalf of fatherhood.

3) Parent education, family education, and family support programs could further family-generated community building by adding more explicit consideration of housing as a productive family asset, as well as food production as an empowering family function. Housing and land are

---

74   Peter Katz, *The New Urbanism: Toward an Architecture of Community* (New York: McGraw Hill), 1994.

critical *capital* assets for families, and it would be a natural extension of the training that family resource programs already offer to add them as subjects. Many family support programs grew out of a legitimate concern for making health and human service programs more respectful toward, and reflective of, the strengths of families.

There has been a growing consensus among those on varying points along the political spectrum that the institution of marriage must be strengthened.[75] Although some scholars and think tanks have come around to a greater respect for marriage, trends do not show any measurable increase in the marriage rate in the population.[76]

The precarious state of marriage will be alleviated in part by giving families more armor to defend themselves against the forces that work incessantly to separate them. Many young people don't believe that they have enough control of their lives to enter into and sustain a marriage. Previous chapters have identified how policies, communities, and parents themselves can thicken and strengthen their roles.

4) Localism is becoming a stronger force in the lives of individuals and families in the United States. More people are choosing where to live based on quality-of-life concerns over the desire to move up career ladders. Continuous geographic mobility is not as attractive as it once was to young and middle-aged adults. The benefits of staying longer in one place include the deepening of friendships, stronger institutional ties, and less disruption to family relationships. When a family is in a place longer, it is able to better organize its productive faculties and assets. It takes time to build a well-functioning, productive habitat. Writers at different points of the political spectrum have analyzed this increase in localism and expect it only to continue as energy prices rise and communications technology breaks down the barriers caused by geographical distances.[77]

5) There are circles in which a concern for strengthening marriage

---

75   David Popenoe and Barbara Dafoe Whitehead, *The State of Our Unions* (Piscataway, NJ: The National Marriage Project, Rutgers, The State University of New Jersey), 2003; Linda J. Waite and Maggie Gallagher, *The Case for Marriage: Why Married People Are Happier, Healthier, and Better Off Financially* (New York: Doubleday), 2000; see also data assembled by Patrick Fagan, Heritage Foundation, www.heritage.org/Research/Family.

76   See recent data that show a continuing decline in the percentages of persons in married households at the US Census Bureau's "America's Families and Living Arrangements," www.census.gov/population/www/socdemo/hh-fam/cps2010.html.

77   Joel Kotkin, *The Next Hundred Million: America in 2050* (New York: Penguin Press), 2010; see also Marvin Olasky, "The Revival of Localism," *World* Magazine, March 12, 2011, cover story, go to www.worldmag.com/articles/17695.

is growing. **Family-generated community building can strengthen boundaries around families and marriages, thereby making marriage a less risky institution to enter. In turn, fostering marital commitments, as the advocates of marriage are doing, can raise the likelihood of successful, durable community building around children.** Productive family institutions can be tools for indirectly strengthening marriage. Thicker roles for mothers and fathers can keep married partners more deeply bonded and along more functional lines. Policies now being advocated for strengthening marriage can themselves be strengthened by policies that also support the productive roles and assets of families.

A large and growing body of advocates (many of whom are themselves fathers) calls for a deeper involvement of fathers in the lives of their children. Some, but not all, of these advocates also promote the return of men to responsible—and where possible, married—relationships with the mothers of their children.

6) There is a growing number of groups dedicated to strengthening fatherhood. Family-generated community building opens up possibilities for fathers to find new, dignified, and manly roles to play in the management of their families and households. In turn, the growing interest in fatherhood fostered by scholars and advocates has brought men back into the family agenda. More men will return to their fatherly roles when they see that there are productive, respectful roles for them to play—roles that make them central rather than marginal partners in the raising of children. Family-generated community building cannot take place without the co-leadership of fathers and mothers; more fathers can be reintegrated into family life through community development that builds productive roles for them.

Despite the obstacles, there is still hope for the productive family. Children need it and in their own ways demand it. Communities have yet to find stability without it. New models for communities must recognize it, and they can be strengthened by doing so.

Families have never abandoned their efforts to strengthen and thicken their productive roles. In defiance of what some analysts would call inevitable evolutionary trends, and in the face of powerful corporations and agencies, mothers and fathers in rural, urban, and suburban localities seem to form new productive enterprises as fast as the older ones fail. The problem is not that they are not desired—it is that they are so difficult to sustain.

Family-generated community building constitutes a multilevel framework for policy development, local planning, and personal role building by parents that can make productive family life more durable. Being productive is a natural human impulse. Expressing that impulse successfully through motherhood and fatherhood not only creates more satisfying experiences for the adults, but also creates healthy examples for children who themselves will eventually become the family builders and community builders needed by coming generations.

CHAPTER 10

The Populist Politics Needed to Sustain Family-Generated Community Building

Family-generated community building evokes a politics rooted in a populist philosophy that was more active at the end of the nineteenth century than it is today. Populism is a view of politics that stresses vesting power in the common people as opposed to the State, powerful corporations, or political elites. The Populist Movement represented the last time major, national political forces were mobilized intentionally on behalf of productive family institutions.

The Populists lost the battle for mainstream party control, but never died out. Their influence peaked before the legendary "realigning election" of 1896.[78] At that time, political interests were realigning around a new progressive regime that effected an accommodation between the business, government, and professional interests whose growth was jointly phasing the family out of most of its productive functions.

Under progressivism, the government assumed the role of regulating corporate excess and corruption, as well as providing universal education for children. Power was vested in professional administrators and, gradually throughout the twentieth century, in human service and education professionals to teach and care for children.

The role relegated to the family that served the interests of business and government was that of consumer. Consumerism became a way of life that celebrated and reinforced the habits that made families dependent on businesses and government for their goods and services.

---

78   Lawrence Goodwyn, *The Populist Moment: A Short History of the Agrarian Revolt in America* (Oxford: Oxford University Press), 1978; Robert C. McMath, Jr., *American Populism: A Social History* (New York: Hill and Wang), 1992.

The progressive compromise between business, government, and professional associations was destabilized by a new regime ushered into power in the 1980 national elections. Although not as deep a realignment as that of 1896, this election did give a strong foothold to a "market" regime that made attacking the power of government's compensatory and regulatory functions its central purpose.[79] However, whereas populists in the nineteenth century resisted government expansion in order to protect their productive institutions, the twentieth century's proponents of the market regime focused on peeling back government in order to vest more power in business corporations.

The market regime—currently still in vogue in American politics—is, like all ideologies, a self-propagating philosophy that redefines families and communities in its own image. One of its progeny, the "choice" movement in education, raises consumerism—in education politics in particular—to its highest profile ever.[80]

Moreover, consumerism emerges as a theme even in defense politics. Shopping in the face of terrorist threats has been extolled by some political leaders as a patriotic act, almost akin to national service. Political electioneering has become almost purely a marketing process involving politicians' creating obsessively crafted sound-bite positions for segments of consumer/voter groups, and then surveying them to ascertain whether their preferences have moved on the margins.

The market regime's proponents speak eloquently about their love for family and community, but tend to ignore exploitation of the latter two by large business corporations. By draining away the legitimacy of government agencies, they help to undermine the progressive compromise that at least had provided some counterbalancing against the destructive effects of corporate decisions on families. In fact, the market philosophy that has been celebrated so widely since 1980 ushered in a raw form of individualism that coincided with an acceleration of what had been an already growing divorce rate.

Progressivism and the market regime have, over the past one hundred years, shifted families out of their own productive institutions and into consumerism and then, in recent years, made consumerism itself a frighteningly unstable way of life. Family debt levels are at their highest ever, but ironically, because they sustain consumption, they provide today's tenuous foundation for economic growth. Unemployment and unstable employment make daily life a scramble to pay bills, avoid bankruptcy, and stave off mortgage foreclosures.

---

79   "Regime" refers here not to a particular presidential administration, but rather to a central organizing principle that impacts comprehensively the design of political institutions and public policies.

80   See John E. Chubb and Terry Moe, *Politics, Markets, and America's Schools* (Washington, D.C.: The Brookings Institution), 1990.

The economic uncertainty and sheer lack of economic opportunity have hit African-American communities so hard that, as scholars put it, vast numbers of men are now considered "unmarriageable."[81] A lack of economic wherewithal opens communities to the inflow of the illicit drug market, shifts control of the streets to gangs, and eventually leads many men and women into prison. As prisons and correctional budgets have grown, the welfare state's support for poor families of all races has been curtailed by proponents of the market regime. However, amid shrinking government benefits and the limited employment markets, the poor do not have their own productive institutions to fall back on to at least feed and shelter themselves.

The policy approach offered to boost growth and create more jobs is to cut taxes and thereby foster more consumerism, the measures of which are now the most highly watched of the nation's indicators of economic health. More "choice" and more spending are the rallying calls of the market regime's policies. But for the poor, the choices and spending opportunities are limited: tax cuts do not help them because they do not increase discretionary spending among the poor, and the jobs created either are unavailable or insufficient to lift them out of poverty. Indeed, many paths lead to drug abuse, participation in the drug economy, and incarceration.

Despite the underlying antipathy of the market regime for small, productive family institutions, the sheer resilience of individuals and families keeps alive the quest to form them. Despite the arrogance exhibited toward families by some education professionals and government agencies, many families fight to maintain their roles as their children's teachers and caregivers. Many seek to make their communities into good places for their children. Some policies exist that support these actions. Many more are needed.

But policies that foster family-generated community building will require a political agenda that is premised on a sound analysis of the political regime that is now in place, plus the mobilization of those whose interests would be served by an expansion of productive family roles and institutions. Moreover, a political program is needed to frame the design of policies.

Historically, any regime active in American politics has contained some mix of populist, progressive, and market sentiments. Populism invests power in small, independent, and sometimes family-owned institutions. Progressivism entrusts professionals—their agencies and bureaucracies, along with enlightened civic organizations—to bring what they hope is a studied, ethical approach to public decision making. Market advocates favor privatizing activities and letting competitive economic forces decide which entities should solve problems.

---

81   William Julius Wilson, *When Work Disappears: The World of the Urban Poor* (New York: Alfred A. Knopf), 1996.

Let us consider these strains, and then elaborate on the kind of populism that is needed in order to foster family-generated community building. The goal here is not to advocate a purely populist regime, but rather a coherent policy approach, one that would enable productive family institutions to flourish in communities alongside the agencies, schools, and businesses that have been the products of progressive and market forces.

Family-generated community building must take place in a context where populist, progressive, and market regime policies are operating in a healthy balance. None of the three represents utopia. Neither is any one of them evil. Each taken to excess can become destructive: populist sentiments can be exploited to foment racial or ethnic resentment among different grass roots groups; progressivism can open the door to elitist domination of government bureaucracies; and the market regime can misapply its philosophy by putting everything up for sale, including public lands, public goods, and all forms of human relationships.[82] Moreover, there is the danger of each strain of politics becoming too dominant and using the "coercive apparatus" of the state—military forces, police, and the prison system—to suppress those who do not embrace its views.

Indeed, each political strain has been invoked at times to justify the oppressive use of governmental power. A populist militarism led Andrew Jackson, in the name of protecting small farmers, to heap untold hardships upon the Cherokee and Seminole Indian tribes in the early nineteenth century. The urban renewal policies of the 1950s could be described as progressive coercion, destroying communities and steering poor, mostly black, citizens into isolated, marginalized public-housing developments. The recent reforms in welfare, coupled with the toughening of sentencing laws, could be characterized as market coercion: the message to the poor is to succeed in the job market as you find it or choose other means of survival (especially drug sales and crime) that will eventually lead to incarceration.

The three-way balance between progressive, market, and populist politics that family-generated community building needs requires the following:

- Policies that support and protect productive family institutions.
- Policies that set boundaries around the capacities of business corporations and government programs that finance them to put family businesses and farms out of existence.
- Policies that ensure that schools and agencies build into their institutional practices new levels of respect and support for

---

82   Robert Kuttner, *Everything for Sale: The Virtues and Limits of Markets* (Chicago: University of Chicago Press), 1996.

productive family roles and coproduction partnerships with families.

- Policies that protect the integrity of communities of place. Healthy communities of place are inherently balanced across the three regimes. Maintaining the viability of places through sound planning and integrated policy approaches would help to sustain the equilibrium.

The above array of policies would necessitate a balance between populist, progressive, and market forces that is not present in today's market-oriented political order, nor was it present during the progressive order, which wielded more influence during most of the twentieth century.

Where would the power base come from to effect such a populist-progressive-market balance? It would need to arise from families, those who identify with their struggle, and from those who see it to be in their interest to work with a thriving, diversified, and productive array of family institutions.

When one looks closely enough at how many families are trying to live, one finds that this impulse to be productive manifests in many contemporary ways. Previous chapters have recounted some of those examples. Although they are not always articulated in such terms (partly because "populism" has become an abused word), these constitute present-day populist aspirations for more control of the family's space, its home, its property, its decisions, its income-generating capacities, its communications with others, its cultural practices, and other aspects of its domain.

Look closely at small town life and one will see families operating businesses. Inspect the workings of urban neighborhoods and there are mothers and fathers working from home, young people composing and performing their own music in their makeshift home studios, and parents coaching their children about their homework subjects in adapted learning spaces. Knock on doors in suburban developments and one will find home offices with parents working online as virtual assistants while they also tend to the meals or maintenance tasks in their homes. Visit rural communities in the south, north, east, or west and there are thousands of families running farms, managing orchards, tending vineyards, and taking care of apiaries, even as they also play leadership roles on local commissions and boards or serve as volunteer firefighters. These families are doing these productive things because they enable them to hold in balance and enrich the various—economic, social, and cultural—domains of their lives. These constitute the irreplaceable capacities that must be operative if communities are to be sustained.

The political base for a renewed kind of populism is out there, but it needs to be galvanized by political leaders who can get to know it, identify with it, and articulate a coherent agenda. Family-generated community building celebrates and mobilizes the capacities that exist at the levels of family, community, and government to restore power to productive family life while updating it in ways that respect the advances achieved by mothers and open new roles for fathers. Hopefully, this book's advocacy of family-generated community building can aid in this task.

Bibliography

Bellah, Robert N., Richard Madsen, William M. Sullivan, Ann Swidler, and Steven M. Tipton. 1985. *Habits of the Heart: Individualism and Commitment in American Life*. Berkeley, CA: University of Californian Press.

Blankenhorn, David. 1995. *Fatherless America*. New York: Basic Books.

Boorstin, Daniel J. and Brooks Mather Kelley. 2002. *A History of the United States*. Needham, MA: Prentice Hall.

Booth, Alan, and Ann C. Crouter. 2001. *Does It Take a Village?* Mahwah, NJ: Lawrence Erlbaum Associates.

Bronfenbrenner, Urie. 1979. *The Ecology of Human Development*. Cambridge, MA: Harvard University Press.

Butterfield, Alice K., Cynthia J. Rocha, and William H. Butterfield. 2010. *The Dynamics of Family Policy: Analysis and Advocacy*. Chicago, IL: Lyceum Press.

Carlson, Allan. 1998. "The State's Assault on the Family," in Christopher Wolfe, ed., *The Family, Civil Society, and the State*. Lanham, Maryland: Rowman and Littlefield.

Chubb, John E. and Terry Moe. 1990. *Politics, Markets, and America's Schools*. Washington, DC: The Brookings Institution.

Comer, James P., Norris M. Haynes, and Edward T. Joyner, 1996. "The School Development Program," in Comer, Haynes, Joyner, and Bev-Avie eds., *Rallying the Whole Village*. New York: Teachers College Press.

David, Laurie, 2010. *The Family Dinner: Great Ways to Connect with Your Kids, One Meal at a Time.* New York, NY: Hachette Book Group.

Dolan, Tom. Live/work Institute website. http://www.live-work.com/lwi/.

Dorgan, B. Summer. 2000. "Farms of the Future." www.futurenet .org/14foodforlife/dorgan.

Durst, Christine and Haaren, Michael. 2005. *The 2-Second Commute.* Franklin Lakes, NJ: Career Press.

Dryfoos, Joy and Sue Maguire. 2002. *Inside Full-Service Community Schools.* Thousand Oaks, CA: Corwin Press, Inc.

Edwards, Paul and Sara Edwards. 1985. *Working from Home: Everything You Need to Know about Living and Working Under the Same Roof.* Los Angeles, CA: Jeremy P. Tarcher, Inc.

———. 2002. *The Entrepreneurial Parent.* New York, NY: Jeremy P. Tarcher/Putnam.

———. 2004. *The Best Home Businesses for People 50+.* New York, NY: Jeremy P. Tarcher/Penguin.

Erikson, Erik H. 1963. *Childhood and Society.* New York: W. W. Norton & Co.

Etzioni, Amitai. 1993. *The Spirit of Community.* New York, NY: Crown Publishers.

Ewers, John C. 1958. *The Blackfeet: Raiders of the Northern Plains.* Norman, OK: University of Oklahoma Press.

Franklin, John Hope, and Alfred A. Moss Jr. 2000. *From Slavery to Freedom: A History of African Americans.* New York: Alfred A. Knopf.

Garbarino, James. 1992. *Children and Families in the Social Environment.* New York: Aldine de Gruyter.

Garbarino, James, Nancy Dubrow, Kathleen Kostelny, and Carole Pardo. 1992. *Children in Danger.* San Francisco, CA: Jossey-Bass Publishers.

Gatto, John Taylor. 1992. *Dumbing Us Down: The Hidden Curriculum of Compulsory Schooling.* Gabriola Island, BC: New Society Publishers.

Gleeson, James P. and Creasie Finney Hairston. 1999. "Kinship Care as a Child Welfare Service: What Do We Really Know?" in James P. Gleeson and Creasie Finney Hairston, eds., *Kinship Care: Improving Practice through Research*. Washington, DC: Child Welfare League of America.

Goodwyn, Lawrence. 1978. *The Populist Moment: A Short History of the Agrarian Revolt in America*. Oxford: Oxford University Press.

Hawkins, J. David, Richard F. Catalano, Jr., and Associates. 1992. *Communities That Care*. San Francisco, CA: Jossey-Bass Publishers.

Hellwig, Maureen. 2002. Illinois Workforce Advantage: An Experiment in Place-Based Government/Community Partnerships. Chicago, IL: Policy Research Action Group, Loyola University.

Hersch, Patricia. 1998. *A Tribe Apart: A Journey into the Heart of American Adolescence*. New York: The Ballantine Publishing Group.

Johnson, Tory and Robert Freedman Spizman. 2008. *Will Work from Home*. New York, NY: Berkeley Books.

Katz, Peter. 1994. *The New Urbanism: Toward an Architecture of Community*. New York: McGraw Hill.

Kim, Hyun Sik. 2011. "Consequences of Parental Divorce for Child Development," *American Sociological Review*. 76 (3), pp. 487—511.

Kordesh, Richard S. 1991. "Community for Children," National Civic Review, Fall, pp. 374–380.

———. 1995. Irony and Hope in the Emerging Family Policies: A Case for Family Empowerment Associations. University Park, PA: Institute for Policy Research and Evaluation.

———. 2006. *Creating and Sustaining Productive Family Habitats*. A study supported by the Annie E. Casey Foundation, Oak Park, IL, February 2006.

———. 2010. "Mistakes in Place: The Premature Termination of Illinois Workforce Advantage," in Giloth, Robert, and Colin Austin, *Mistakes to Success: Learning and Adapting When Things Go Wrong*. New York, NY: iUniverse, pp. 185–203.

Kordesh, Richard S. and Robert Constable. 2002. "Policies, Programs, and Mandates for Developing Social Services in Schools," in Robert

Constable, Shirley McDonald, and John P. Flynn, eds., *School Social Work: Practice, Policy, and Research Perspectives.* Chicago, IL: Lyceum Press, pp. 83–100.

Kotkin, Joel. 2010. *The Next Hundred Million: America in 2050.* New York, NY: The Penguin Press.

Kuttner, Robert. 1996. *Everything for Sale: The Virtues and Limits of Markets.* Chicago: University of Chicago Press.

Lukes, Steven. 1974. *Power: A Radical View.* London: MacMillan Press.

McMath, Robert C. Jr. 1992. *American Populism: A Social History.* New York: Hill and Wang.

McKenzie, Evan. 1994. *Privatopias: Homeowner Associations and the Rise of Residential Private Government.* New Haven, CT: Yale University Press.

Michigan Department of Education. 2002. "What Research Says about Parent Involvement in Children's Education in Relation to Academic Achievement." East Lansing, MI. March.

National Center for Family and Community Connections with Schools. 2002. Research Brief, November.

National Longitudinal Survey of Youth, National Longitudinal Survey of Adolescent Health, 1995, 1996.

Olasky, Marvin. "The Revival of Localism." In *World Magazine,* March, 12, 2011; cover story. http://www.worldmag.com/articles/17695.

Ooms, Theodora. 1996. "Where is the Family in Comprehensive Community Initiatives for Children and Families?" Washington, DC: Family Impact Seminar.

Pitts, Leonard. "Abundant Blessings for the Royal Newlyweds." *Chicago Tribune,* April 28, 2011; 17.

Parke, Mary. 2003. "Are Married Parents Really Better for Children?" Washington, DC: Center for Law and Social Policy. Policy Brief No. 3, May.

Popenoe, David. 1988. *Disturbing the Nest: Family Change and Decline in Modern Societies.* Hawthorne, MA: Aldine de Gruyter.

Popenoe, David and Barbara Dafoe Whitehead. 2003. *The State of Our Unions, 2003.* Piscataway, NJ: The National Marriage Project, Rutgers, The State University of New Jersey.

Pratt, Joanne H. 1999. *Home-Based Business: The Hidden Economy: A Report from 125,000 Women, Men, Black, Hispanic, and Other Minority Entrepreneurs.* A study carried out for the Office of Advocacy, US Small Business Administration, Washington, DC.

Robyn, Kathryn L. and Dawn Ritchie. 2005. *The Emotional House: How Redesigning Your Home Can Change Your Life.* Oakland, CA: New Harbinger Publications.

Roberts, Dorothy. 2002. *Shattered Bonds: The Color of Child Welfare.* New York: Basic Civitas Books.

Segalen, Martine. 1996. "The Industrial Revolution: From Proletariat to Bourgeoisie," in André Burguiére, Christiane Klapisch-Zuber, Martine Segalen & Francoise Zonabend, eds., *A History of the Family: Volume II: The Impact of Modernity.* Cambridge, MA: Harvard University Press.

Tocqueville, Alexis de. 1956. *Democracy in America.* New York: Mentor Books.

Tönnies, Ferdinand. 1957. *Community and Society.* East Lansing, MI: Michigan State University Press. Originally published in 1887 as *Gemeinschaft und Gesellschaft.*

US Bureau of the Census. 2010. "American's Family and Living Arrangements, 2010." www.census.gov/population/www/socdemo/hh-fam/cps2010.html.

Waite, Linda J. and Maggie Gallagher. 2000. *The Case for Marriage: Why Married People are Happier, Healthier, and Better Off Financially.* New York: Doubleday.

Wallerstein, Judith S., Julia M. Lewis, and Sandra Blakeslee. 2000. *The Unexpected Legacy of Divorce.* New York: Hyperion.

Weinstein, Miriam. 2006. *The Surprising Power of Family Meals: How Eating Together Makes Us Smarter, Stronger, Healthier and Happier.* Hanover, New Hampshire: Steerforth Press, L.C.

Whitehead, Barbara Defoe, and David Popenoe. 2002. *Why Men Won't Commit: Exploring Young Men's Attitudes About Sex, Dating, and Marriage.* Piscataway, NJ: The National Marriage Project. http://www.virginia.edu/marriageproject/.

Williamson, Thad, David Imbroscio, and Gar Alperovitz. 2002. *Making a Place for Community: Local Democracy in a Local Era.* New York: Routledge.

Wilson, William Julius. 1996. *When Work Disappears: The World of the Urban Poor.* New York: Alfred A. Knopf.

About Richard S. Kordesh

RICHARD KORDESH has studied, led projects for, taught about, and written about productive families and their communities for over twenty years. He has done so from governors' offices, universities, and with the support of a number of major foundations. Richard's views of the productive family and its importance to community building are shaped not only by his work, but by his life as a father and husband. He is the father of four children. He has worked from home during several stretches of his career in order to stay closely involved with them. He coached his sons for nine years in youth baseball, he home schooled two of his sons, and with his wife, Maureen, cultivates an extensive vegetable and fruit garden on the family grounds. His interest in families has broadened from the United States to a global level. In recent years, he has trained graduate students and community workers in Ethiopia about methods for strengthening their families through productive uses of their habitats. Richard's master's degree in social work trained him as a grass-roots community developer. His PhD in political science has allowed him to research, teach, and publish about the larger political and economic forces that affect families and the communities where they live.

For updates on family-generated community building, please visit www.bluehouseinstitute.com

Index

www.ingramcontent.com/pod-product-compliance
Lightning Source LLC
Chambersburg PA
CBHW061306280526
45784CB00002B/914